CONSTITUTIONAL
AMENDMENTS
BEYOND THE BILL OF RIGHTS

Amendments XVIII and XXI Prohibition and Repeal

Other Books of Related Interest

Opposing Viewpoints Series

Civil Liberties

Feminism

Race Relations

Work

Working Women

Current Controversies Series

Civil Liberties

Extremist Groups

Feminism

Human Rights

CONSTITUTIONAL
AMENDMENTS
BEYOND THE BILL OF RIGHTS

Amendments XVIII and XXI
Prohibition and Repeal

Sylvia Engdahl, Book Editor

GREENHAVEN PRESS
A part of Gale, Cengage Learning

GALE
CENGAGE Learning™

Detroit • New York • San Francisco • New Haven, Conn • Waterville, Maine • London

Christine Nasso, *Publisher*
Elizabeth Des Chenes, *Managing Editor*

© 2009 Greenhaven Press, a part of Gale, Cengage Learning.

Gale and Greenhaven Press are registered trademarks used herein under license.

For more information, contact:
Greenhaven Press
27500 Drake Rd.
Farmington Hills, MI 48331-3535
Or you can visit our Internet site at gale.cengage.com

For product information and technology assistance, contact us at

Gale Customer Support, 1-800-877-4253
For permission to use material from this text or product, submit all requests online at www.cengage.com/permissions

Further permissions questions can be emailed to permissionrequest@cengage.com

Articles in Greenhaven Press anthologies are often edited for length to meet page require-ments. In addition, original titles of these works are changed to clearly present the main thesis and to explicitly indicate the author's opinion. Every effort is made to ensure that Greenhaven Press accurately reflects the original intent of the authors. Every effort has been made to trace the owners of copyrighted material.

Cover photograph © Archive Photos/Getty Images.

LIBRARY OF CONGRESS CATALOGING-IN-PUBLICATION DATA

Amendments XVIII and XXI : prohibition and repeal / Sylvia Engdahl, book editor.
    p. cm. -- (Constitutional amendments: beyond the Bill of Rights)
    Includes bibliographical references and index.
    ISBN 978-0-7377-4328-9 (hardcover)
    1. Prohibition--United States--History--20th century--Sources. 2. Liquor laws--United States--History--20th century--Sources. 3. United States. Constitution. 18th Amendment. 4. United States. Constitution. 21st Amendment. I. I. Engdahl, Sylvia. II. II. Title: Amendments 18 and 21. III. III. Title: Amendments Eighteen and Twenty-one.
    KF3919.A844 2009
    344.7305'41--dc22

                                                            2008051451

Printed in the United States of America
1 2 3 4 5 6 7 13 12 11 10 09

Contents

Chapter 1: Historical Background on the Eighteenth and Twenty-first Amendments

Chapter 2: Impact of Amendment XVIII on Constitutional Law

Chapter 3: Impact of Amendment XXI on Constitutional Law

Chapter 4: Current Relevance of Amendments XVIII and XXI

Appendices

Prohibition and Repeal

> *"Today's Constitution is a realistic document of freedom only because of several corrective amendments. Those amendments speak to a sense of decency and fairness."*
>
> *Thurgood Marshall*

While the U.S. Constitution forms the backbone of American democracy, the amendments make the Constitution a living, ever-evolving document. Interpretation and analysis of the Constitution inform lively debate in every branch of government, as well as among students, scholars, and all other citizens, and views on various articles of the Constitution have changed over the generations. Formally altering the Constitution, however, can happen only through the amendment process. The Greenhaven Press series The Bill of Rights examines the first ten amendments to the Constitution. Constitutional Amendments: Beyond the Bill of Rights continues the exploration, addressing key amendments ratified since 1791.

The process of amending the Constitution is painstaking. While other options are available, the method used for nearly every amendment begins with a congressional bill that must pass both the Senate and the House of Representatives by a two-thirds majority. Then the amendment must be ratified by three-quarters of the states. Many amendments have been proposed since the Bill of Rights was adopted in 1791, but only seventeen have been ratified.

It may be difficult to imagine a United States where women and African Americans are prohibited from voting, where the federal government allows one human being to enslave another, or where some citizens are denied equal protection under the law. While many of our most fundamental liberties are protected by the Bill of Rights, the amendments that followed have significantly broadened and enhanced the rights of American citizens. Such rights may be taken for granted today, but when the amendments were ratified, many were considered groundbreaking and proved to be explosively controversial.

Each volume in Constitutional Amendments provides an in-depth exploration of an amendment and its impact through primary and secondary sources, both historical and contemporary. Primary sources include landmark Supreme Court rulings, speeches by prominent experts, and newspaper editorials. Secondary sources include historical analyses, law journal articles, book excerpts, and magazine articles. Each volume first presents the historical background of the amendment, creating a colorful picture of the circumstances surrounding the amendment's passage: the campaigns to sway public opinion, the congressional debates, and the struggle for ratification. Next, each volume examines the ways the court system has been used to test the validity of the amendment and addresses the ramifications of the amendment's passage. The final chapter of each volume presents viewpoints that explore current controversies and debates relating to ways in which the amendment affects our everyday lives.

Numerous features are included in each Constitutional Amendments volume:

- An originally written introduction presents a concise yet thorough overview of the amendment.

- A time line provides historical context by describing key events, organizations, and people relating to the ratification of the amendment, subsequent court cases, and the impact of the amendment.

- An annotated table of contents offers an at-a-glance summary of each primary and secondary source essay included in the volume.

- The complete text of the amendment, followed by a "plain English" explanation, brings the amendment into clear focus for students and other readers.

- Graphs, charts, tables, and maps enhance the text.

- A list of all twenty-seven Constitutional Amendments offers quick reference.

- An annotated list of court cases relevant to the amendment broadens the reader's understanding of the judiciary's role in interpreting the Constitution.

- A bibliography of books, periodicals, and Web sites aids readers in further research.

- A detailed subject index allows readers to quickly find the information they need.

With the aid of this series, students and other researchers will become better informed of their rights and responsibilities as American citizens. Constitutional Amendments: Beyond the Bill of Rights examines the roots of American democracy, bringing to life the ways the Constitution has evolved and how it has impacted this nation's history.

Amendment Texts and Explanations

The Eighteenth Amendment to the Constitution

Passed by Congress December 18, 1917. Ratified January 16, 1919. Repealed by Amendment XXI.

Section 1. After one year from the ratification of this article the manufacture, sale, or transportation of intoxicating liquors within, the importation thereof into, or the exportation thereof from the United States and all territory subject to the jurisdiction thereof for beverage purposes is hereby prohibited.

Section 2. The Congress and the several States shall have concurrent power to enforce this article by appropriate legislation.

Section 3. This article shall be inoperative unless it shall have been ratified as an amendment to the Constitution by the legislatures of the several States, as provided in the Constitution, within seven years from the date of the submission hereof to the States by the Congress.

Explanation

The Eighteenth Amendment to the Constitution prohibits the manufacture, sale, or transportation of intoxicating liquor, and the import or export of liquor, within the United States and its territories, starting one year from the ratification of this article. Both Congress and the states shall have the power to pass laws to enforce this article.

The Twenty-first Amendment to the Constitution

Passed by Congress February 20, 1933. Ratified December 5, 1933.

Section 1. The eighteenth article of amendment to the Constitution of the United States is hereby repealed.

Section 2. The transportation or importation into any State, Territory, or Possession of the United States for delivery or use therein of intoxicating liquors, in violation of the laws thereof, is hereby prohibited.

Section 3. This article shall be inoperative unless it shall have been ratified as an amendment to the Constitution by conventions in the several States, as provided in the Constitution, within seven years from the date of the submission hereof to the States by the Congress.

Explanation

The Eighteenth Amendment is hereby repealed. The transportation or importation of intoxicating liquor into any state, territory, or possession of the United States is hereby prohibited if the liquor is intended for delivery or use in violation of that state or territory's laws.

Introduction

For a short period in the early twentieth century—just under fourteen years—the manufacture and sale of alcoholic beverages was illegal in the United States. This period is known as the Prohibition era. Despite its brevity, Prohibition had far-reaching effects on American society and on the relationship between Americans and the federal government—effects that involved much more than the issue of whether or not people should be allowed to drink liquor. Those effects are still being felt today.

The prohibition of alcohol was not a sudden event. Throughout the nineteenth century, and especially during its second half, there had been a growing temperance movement. Temperance originally meant moderation in the use of alcohol, but in the eyes of most supporters it eventually came to mean abolishing it entirely. Many churches exhorted people not to drink, but preaching against the evils of alcohol was not confined to churches. Long, emotional books and speeches on the subject were common. The schools taught that alcohol itself, not merely the abuse of it, was harmful. And so one by one, states passed prohibition laws of their own. The first to do so was Maine in 1851, and by the time national Prohibition went into effect in 1920, thirty-three states, covering 63 percent of the U.S. population, were already "dry."

One reason for the strong opposition to alcohol was its association with saloons. The saloons that existed before Prohibition were disreputable places. Middle-class men did not patronize them. Respectable women never entered them, except occasionally as crusaders agitating for their destruction. Working-class men who visited them were all too likely to spend long hours there, get drunk, and neglect or abuse their families; antialcohol publicity often featured the starving children of fathers who spent their wages on drink. Moreover, saloons were centers of gambling, prostitution, and political corruption, gathering places for crooked officials and police who were bribed to disregard violations of local laws. It was commonly thought that eliminating saloons would bring about a dramatic reduction in crime. The Anti-Saloon League, founded in 1893, became the most powerful of the organizations that lobbied for Prohibition, and it gained widespread support.

Another factor that led to national Prohibition was America's entry into World War I. Many people believed that drinking was immoral and thus incompatible with the high ideals that underlay public support for the "War to End All Wars." The sale of liquor to soldiers was forbidden, and eventually the use of grain to manufacture alcoholic beverages was banned as a wartime measure to reserve cereal grains for food for the troops. The public, dedicated to the war effort, was in a mood to make sacrifices. Furthermore, many beer brewers were of German descent, and agitators against breweries exploited the strong anti-German sentiment that existed during the war years.

All these factors combined to create a public demand for Prohibition to become nationwide and permanent. But Congress did not have authority to pass a national Prohibition law because making laws that controlled what individual citizens could do, as opposed to what government could do, was not among the powers authorized by the Constitution. Today, ways around this restriction have been developed—many things, such as illegal drugs, are forbidden through the federal government's power to control interstate commerce. But at the time that Prohibition was proposed, most legal experts believed that alcohol could be banned only by a constitutional amendment. Such an amendment was first considered by Congress in 1914, but failed to receive the two-thirds majority vote needed for it to pass. When it was introduced again, in 1917, it did pass and was submitted to the states for ratification. It became the Eighteenth Amendment when ratified in 1919, and went into effect one year later, on January 16, 1920.

The result was not what people had expected. As journalist Herbert Asbury wrote in his 1950 book *The Great Illusion,*

> For more than a hundred years they had been indoctrinated with the idea that the destruction of the liquor traffic was the will of God and would provide the answers to most, if not all, of mankind's problems. . . . They had expected to be greeted, when the great day came, by a covey of angels bearing gifts of peace, happiness, prosperity, and salvation, which they had been assured would be theirs when the rum demon had been scotched. Instead they were met by a horde of bootleggers, moonshiners, rumrunners, hijackers, gangsters, racketeers, trigger men, venal judges, corrupt police, crooked politicians, and speakeasy operators, all bearing the twin symbols of the Eighteenth Amendment—the tommy gun and the poisoned cup.

Supporters of Prohibition believed that it would be relatively easy to enforce. They did not foresee the reaction of the public to federal restrictions on private conduct. Adoption of such restrictions was an extremely radical step—a 1926 editorial in the *New Republic* called it "the most radical political and social experiment of our day"—and many citizens, even those who had not previously been heavy drinkers, resented it. Laws affecting individuals had in the past been made only at the local and state level—even the income tax, which had not been introduced until 1913, was imposed only on the wealthy. By now, everyone is used to the idea of ordinary people's actions being regulated by federal laws. It was Prohibition that brought about this change in outlook. Unfortunately, it also brought about a lasting attitude of disrespect for the law in general.

It might be thought that because so many states already had prohibition laws, the majority of the population would not have cared. But the dry states were predominantly rural, agricultural ones. The attitude in big cities, especially those containing large numbers of immigrants from countries where moderate drinking was an integral part of the culture, was quite different. Also, people who wanted liquor in dry states could no longer have it shipped to them, a practice that under many state laws—those intended merely to abolish saloons—had been legal. So the market for bootleg liquor was large, and it led to the rise of organized crime, a new phenomenon that arose to meet the demand and has continued to thrive ever since.

Notorious gangsters such as Al Capone gained wealth and power beyond anything previously imagined, and by many they were viewed as celebrities. Violence as well as illegal trafficking became rampant. Shoot-outs—between rival gangs, between federal agents and gangsters, and between the Coast Guard and rumrunners—became common. Police and federal law enforcement officers made little headway in stemming the liquor traffic, and a good many of them were corrupted by bribes. The federal courts were overwhelmed; a 1931 government document observed, "The effect of the huge volume of liquor prosecutions, which has come to these courts under prohibition, has injured their dignity, impaired their efficiency, and endangered the wholesome respect for them which once obtained. Instead of being impressive tribunals of superior jurisdiction, they have had to do the work of police courts."

Lack of respect for courts and for corrupt officials, however, was minor compared to the prevailing lack of respect for the Prohibition law itself. Previously, most people had considered themselves law-abiding citizens. Now flouting the law became socially acceptable. This was partly due to the obvious hypocrisy of the numerous government officials, such as President Warren G. Harding, who were known to drink bootleg liquor behind closed doors. But it was mainly the result of the excitement and glamour attached to forbidden drinking. People who had once drunk only wine with meals now went to speakeasies and drank cocktails. It was estimated that there were over a hundred thousand speakeasies (illegal bars that required a password for admittance) in New York alone. The speakeasies, unlike the old saloons, were patronized by women as well as men. Few middle-class women had drunk hard liquor before; under Prohibition doing so became fashionable.

Contrary to a common belief, the Eighteenth Amendment did not prohibit possession or consumption of liquor, although some state laws did. Only the manufacture, sale, and transportation of alcohol was banned under federal law. The National Prohibition Act, known as the Volstead Act, specifically stated that it was legal to drink in private homes (any liquor found elsewhere was presumed to be for sale) and to offer drinks to bona fide guests. Thus people who could afford to do so stocked up before the effective date of the amendment, and were able to smuggle bootleg liquor into their homes later. But the poor, who were accustomed to drinking beer, were unable get it. Bootleggers did not deal in beer, since distilled liquor was easier to produce and transport and, because of its higher alcohol content, was far more profitable. Many people therefore came to feel that the Volstead Act discriminated against the poor. Most supporters of the Eighteenth Amendment had not expected beer and wine to be covered by the law; they were stunned when Congress set the maximum amount of alcohol allowed in a beverage at a mere one-half of 1 percent. Although after the first few months it became legal to make "fruit juices"—i.e., cider and wine—in the home for home consumption, this was not practical for most people and did little to help the situation caused by what many considered an overzealous use of the power given to Congress by the amendment.

With the dramatic rise in crime during the Prohibition Era came a need for stronger measures against it than had previously been considered acceptable. Enforcement officials, desperate for a way to cope with the ever-increasing liquor traffic, turned to methods that many people believed were unconstitutional under the Fourth and Fifth Amendments. The Supreme Court, too, tended to feel that enforcement of Prohibition had top priority. Thus it upheld first the search of automobiles without a warrant, and then the use of wiretapping by government agents—practices originally adopted to catch bootleggers that have become routine today in combating drug dealers and terrorists. The crisis provoked by Prohibition weakened Americans' reluctance to allow such measures. Whether the impact on the rights of innocent citizens can be justified is still being debated.

In the late 1920s, when it became apparent that Prohibition was not working and was in fact creating worse problems than those it was intended to solve, a movement toward repeal of the Eighteenth Amendment began to grow. But the majority of citizens still supported the amendment, at least publicly. Some blamed the problems on liquor itself rather than on what people were doing to obtain it, and held to the belief that the desire to drink could eventually be stamped out. Others simply thought that abstention from alcohol was a moral issue and that the government ought to stand firm for morality. Residents of agricultural states, who had not come into personal contact with the crime that flourished in the cities and along the Canadian border, did not perceive the law as harmful. And dedicated members of the Anti-Saloon League did not want to admit defeat.

At the close of 1927, the Association Against the Prohibition Amendment (AAPA), which had been dormant since the amendment's ratification, decided to launch a campaign for repeal. In 1929 it was joined by the newly formed Women's Organization for National Prohibition Reform (WONPR), which emphasized the dangers that Prohibition-related crime posed to children. These two organizations were instrumental in raising support for repeal. Yet as late as 1931, the Wickersham Commission Report on Alcohol Prohibition, which stated in detail how Prohibition was failing, recommended that it be retained.

However, another issue arose during the Great Depression. Before the Eighteenth Amendment's adoption, the government had derived a large percentage of its revenue from liquor taxes. With times hard and funds scarce, that revenue was needed again. People who favored Prohibition in principle began to feel that it was costing the government too much money. Then in July of 1932, the immensely popular Franklin D. Roosevelt, to whom many people looked for help in ending the Depression, advocated repeal in his speech accepting the Democratic Party's presidential nomination. That turned the tide. Repeal was a feature of his campaign platform and became a significant factor in the Democrats' rise to power. Shortly after President Roosevelt took office, Congress passed a bill legalizing beer and wine. The Twenty-first Amendment, which repealed the eighteenth, soon followed. The bill creating it was passed by Congress only six days after its introduction.

"It was as if someone were opening a bottle of champagne," wrote historian David Kyvig in *Repealing Prohibition*. "At first the cork moved slowly and only under great pressure. But once it reached a certain point, the cork literally exploded out of the neck. The final stage in the complicated process, state approval [ratification] of a new amendment, was completed more quickly than in any previous constitutional change in the nation's history." On December 5, 1933, Roosevelt issued a presidential proclamation announcing the end of national Prohibition, and what had once been called the "noble experiment" passed into history.

Today, some historians say that Prohibition succeeded because liquor consumption fell. But this assessment depends on what is meant by "succeeded." As *Reason* magazine editor Radley Balko has written in its blog, "To call alcohol prohibition a 'success,' one would have to consider overall consumption of alcohol in America the *only* relevant criteria. You'd have to ignore the precipitous rise in homicides and other violent crime; the rise in hospitalizations due to alcohol poisoning; the number of people blinded or killed by drinking toxic, black market gin; the corrupting influence on government officials, from beat cops to the halls of Congress to [President] Harding's attorney general; and the erosion of the rule of law." Defenders mention that there was a significant drop in deaths from cirrhosis of the liver, a disease caused by alcoholism. In reply, critics point out that this drop was offset by the blindness, paralysis and death suffered by thousands of victims who drank denatured industrial alcohol, either intentionally, or unknowingly when bootleggers mixed it with liquor to stretch the supply.

The majority of Americans, both at the time the Twenty-first Amendment was adopted and since, have believed that the attempt to ban alcoholic beverages was a tragic failure, and that it demonstrated the impossibility of trying to change human nature by government decree. Many also consider it responsible for the subsequent pushing of drugs by the crime syndicates it created. The question of whether its long-term effects have harmed the nation is a controversial one.

Chronology

1887

The Supreme Court rules in *Mugler v. Kansas* that states have the power to pass and enforce prohibition laws. Two have already done so, and by the time the Eighteenth Amendment goes into effect, thirty-three states, covering 63 percent of the total population, are "dry."

1890

Congress enacts the Wilson Original Packages Act, which provides that all intoxicating beverages shipped interstate will be subject to the laws of the destination state upon arrival. It does not authorize federal enforcement.

1893

On May 24 the Anti-Saloon League is founded by Howard H. Russell and becomes a major force in raising support for national Prohibition.

1913

On March 1 Congress passes the Webb-Kenyon Act over the veto of President William H. Taft, who believes it to be unconstitutional due to conflict with the Constitution's commerce clause. This law prohibits interstate transportation of liquor if it is intended to be sold, used, or possessed in a state where that is unlawful.

On December 10 the Committee of One Thousand presents a proposed Amendment for National Prohibition to Congress.

1914

On December 22 the House of Representatives votes 197 to 190 for national Prohibition, falling short of the necessary two-thirds majority required to pass.

1917

On January 8 the Supreme Court rules that the Webb-Kenyon Act is constitutional.

On March 3 the Reed "bone-dry" amendment to a post office appropriation bill becomes law, prohibiting personal importation of liquor into states that prohibit its manufacture and sale even when those states allow individuals to bring it in for personal use. It also bans alcohol advertising in such states; however, there is no provision for federal enforcement.

On April 4 the bill that is to become the Eighteenth Amendment is introduced in Congress.

On May 18 Congress prohibits the sale of intoxicating liquor to soldiers, and on October 6 extends this prohibition to the navy.

On August 1 the Eighteenth Amendment bill is passed by the Senate.

On August 10, as a war measure, Congress prohibits the use of foodstuff or feeds in production of distilled spirits for beverages.

On December 8, also as a war measure designed to reserve food, the president prohibits the production of most beer.

On December 18, after passing in the House on the previous day, the final version of the Eighteenth Amendment is adopted by the Senate and submitted to the states for ratification.

1918

On January 8 the Eighteenth Amendment is ratified by Missouri, the first state to do so.

On September 6 the Agricultural Appropriation Act is passed, prohibiting manufacture of beer and wine after May 1, 1919, and forbidding sale of any liquor after June 30, 1919.

On November 12 the Association Against the Prohibition Amendment (AAPA) is founded by William H. Stayton. This organization is later to be instrumental in bringing about repeal.

On November 21, ten days after the World War I armistice, President Wilson signs the Wartime Prohibition Act (passed by Congress on August 29), which prohibits the use of foodstuff to produce any form of alcoholic beverage until the end of demobilization.

1919

On January 16 the Eighteenth Amendment is ratified by Nebraska, the last state needed for it to become law. It is formally certified as ratified on January 29.

On July 1 the Wartime Prohibition Act goes into effect.

On October 28 Congress passes the National Prohibition Act, also known as the Volstead Act, over President Woodrow Wilson's veto.

1920

On January 6 the Supreme Court rules that although beer containing a mere one-half of 1 percent alcohol is not intoxicating and the Eighteenth Amendment concerns only intoxicating beverages, banning it under the Volstead Act is legal because it is incidental to the general power to ban beer.

On January 16 the Eighteenth Amendment and the Volstead Act go into effect. (Not January 29 as some sources erroneously state, having confused the day of the previous year on which ratification was certified with the day on which it went into effect.)

On June 7, in a group of lawsuits known as the national prohibition cases, the Supreme Court rules that the Eighteenth Amendment does not violate any provisions of the Constitution.

On July 24 the Bureau of Internal Revenue issues a ruling lifting the ban on home brewing of cider and wine containing more than one-half of 1 percent alcohol, provided it is "nonintoxicating in fact" and is consumed only in the home.

1923

On April 30 the Supreme Court rules that the Eighteenth Amendment applies to both domestic and foreign ships while in U.S. waters, and that therefore liquor carried into U.S. waters by foreign ships can be seized even if sealed for use elsewhere. This means passenger ships have to dump any liquor not consumed during the voyage overboard before reaching port. The Court also holds, however, that American ships are not subject to Prohibition laws when on the high seas or in foreign ports, which allows them to compete successfully with foreign ships and which leads to the birth of the cruise industry.

1925

On March 2 the Supreme Court rules in *Carroll v. United States* that automobiles can be searched without a warrant if there is probable cause to believe they are transporting liquor.

1926

In April congressional hearings on the National Prohibition Act are held, at which it is argued that beer and wine would be legal under the Eighteenth Amendment and that the law should be modified to allow them.

On May 8 President Calvin Coolidge issues an executive order making state, county, and municipal officers federal officials for enforcing the Prohibition law.

On November 29 the Supreme Court rules that Congress has the power to regulate prescription of wine and spirituous liquor for medicinal purposes. This is a controversial decision viewed by much of the public as a violation of physicians' rights.

1927

On March 3 Congress passes the Bureau of Prohibition Act, effective April 1, which moves enforcement from the Bureau of Internal Revenue to the new bureau, both offices of the Department of the Treasury. It places Prohibition field agents under Civil Service, and 59 percent of them fail the Civil Service examination.

On December 12, a group of prominent men meet and decide to revive the Association Against the Prohibition Amendment and launch a campaign for repeal, although it seems unlikely to succeed.

1928

On June 4, in its ruling in *Olmstead v. United States*, the Supreme Court upholds the use of warrantless wiretapping as a means of obtaining evidence against bootleggers, even when wiretapping is illegal in the state in which it is done. Thus, Prohibition agents are, in effect, authorized to break the law.

In the presidential election Alfred E. Smith, who favors repeal, opposes Herbert Hoover, a strong supporter of Prohibition. Despite the public's waning support for Prohibition, Hoover wins.

1929

On March 22 the Canadian rumrunner *I'm Alone* is sunk by the U.S. Coast Guard in waters beyond American jurisdiction, setting off an international incident.

On May 8 the Women's Organization for National Prohibition Reform (WONPR) is founded by Pauline Sabin, who later appears on the cover of *Time* magazine for July 18, 1932. The organization opposes Prohibition on grounds that its effects are harmful to the young.

1931

The Wickersham Commission Report on Alcohol Prohibition is published on January 7. It points out that enforcement is failing, but nevertheless opposes repeal.

1932

On July 2 in his speech accepting the Democratic Party's nomination for president of the United States, Franklin D. Roosevelt endorses repeal of the Eighteenth Amendment, congratulating the convention for having made repeal part of the party's platform. This has a significant effect on public opinion.

1933

On February 14 the bill proposing the Twenty-first Amendment is introduced into Congress. It is passed by the Senate two days later and by the House four days after that.

On March 23 President Franklin D. Roosevelt signs into law an amendment to the Volstead Act known as the Cullen-Harrison Act, which allows the manufacture and sale of light beer and light wine. Sale of beer resumes on April 7.

On April 10 Michigan ratifies the Twenty-first Amendment, the first state to do so.

On December 5 the Twenty-first Amendment is ratified by Utah, the last state needed, and national Prohibition ends. (However, as the amendment gives the states the right to make their own liquor laws, in some states prohibition of alcohol continues.) Roosevelt issues a presidential proclamation announcing repeal and urging the American people to buy liquor only from licensed dealers, to observe state prohibition laws, to oppose the return of the saloon, and to avoid using alcohol excessively.

1936

In the first of many cases involving conflicts between state power to regulate liquor shipments under the Twenty-first Amendment and federal power to regulate interstate commerce, the Supreme Court rules that a state can exact a license fee for the privilege of importing beer from other states, although prior to the amendment this would have been illegal under the commerce clause.

1966

Mississippi becomes the last state to repeal statewide prohibition of alcohol.

1972

On December 5 the Supreme Court rules in *California v. LaRue* that under the Twenty-first Amendment, states have the right to refuse liquor licenses to establishments offering sexually explicit entertainment even though to forbid such entertainment by law would violate the First Amendment right to free speech.

1976

On December 20 the Supreme Court rules in *Craig v. Boren* that although the Twenty-first Amendment gives the power to regulate liquor sales to the states, it does not override the equal protection clause of the Fourteenth Amendment, and that states therefore cannot set different drinking ages for men and women.

1984

On July 17 Congress passes the National Minimum Drinking Age Act, which reduces the federal highway funds given to states that fail to raise their drinking age to twenty-one. It does not directly set a national drinking age, which would not be legal under the Twenty-first Amendment.

1987

Kansas becomes the last state to repeal its law against selling liquor by the drink.

On June 23 the Supreme Court rules in *South Dakota v. Dole* that although the Twenty-first Amendment gives the right to regulate the sale of alcohol to the states, it does not prevent the federal government from setting conditions involving that sale, and that therefore the National Minimum Drinking Age Act of 1984 is not unconstitutional.

1998

On June 9 Congress enacts the Transportation Equity Act for the 21st Century (TEA-21) which, among things, provides incentives for states to prohibit possession of open alcoholic beverage containers in automobiles. States that do not comply have a percentage of their federal highway funds transferred each year to alcohol education funding.

2005

On May 16 the Supreme Court rules in *Granholm v. Heald* that although the Twenty-first Amendment gives states the power to ban all direct shipment of liquor to consumers, they may not discriminate against out-of-state wineries by allowing only shipments from within the state—a decision applauded by people wishing to buy wine on the Internet.

CONSTITUTIONAL
AMENDMENTS
BEYOND THE BILL OF RIGHTS

CHAPTER 1

Historical Background on the Eighteenth and Twenty-first Amendments

A Constitutional Amendment Is Needed to Ensure Permanent Nationwide Prohibition of Liquor

Richmond P. Hobson

Richmond P. Hobson was a U.S. representative from Alabama who served in Congress from 1905 to 1915. Previously he had been a rear admiral in the U.S. Navy and was later awarded the Medal of Honor for his heroism in the Spanish-American War. He has been called the Father of American Prohibition because he advocated criminalization of alcohol and other drugs, a subject on which he wrote several books. In the following excerpt from the concluding portion of a very long speech describing the evils of alcohol, he expresses his strong opposition to the sale of liquor and his belief that its prohibition must not only be nationwide, but must be placed in the Constitution. This, in his opinion, would ensure that it could never be repealed by Congress in the future; the possibility that a constitutional amendment might be repealed did not occur to him. Immediately following this speech on December 22, 1914, the House of Representatives voted on a resolution calling for such an amendment. Known as the Hobson-Sheppard Resolution, it passed by a narrow margin, lacking the two-thirds majority needed for it to be enacted.

Science has ... demonstrated that alcohol is a protoplasmic poison, poisoning all living things; that alcohol is a habit-forming drug that shackles millions of our citizens and maintains slavery in our midst; that it lowers in a fearful way the standard of efficiency of the Nation, reducing enormously the

Richmond P. Hobson, speech before the U.S. House of Representatives, December 22, 1914.

national wealth, entailing startling burdens of taxation, encumbering the public with the care of crime, pauperism, and insanity; that it corrupts politics and public servants, corrupts the Government, corrupts the public morals, lowers terrifically the average standard of character of the citizenship, and undermines the liberties and institutions of the Nation; that it undermines and blights the home and the family, checks education, attacks the young when they are entitled to protection, undermines the public health, slaughtering, killing, and wounding our citizens many fold times more than war, pestilence, and famine combined; that it blights the progeny of the Nation, flooding the land with a horde of degenerates; that it strikes deadly blows at the life of the Nation itself and at the very life of the race, reversing the great evolutionary principles of nature and the purposes of the Almighty.

There can be but one verdict, and that is this great destroyer must be destroyed. The time is ripe for fulfillment. The present generation, the generation to which we belong, must cut this millstone of degeneracy from the neck of humanity.

The Remedy

What is the remedy for this great organic disease that is Nation-wide and world-wide in its blight? Evidently the treatment must itself be organic and must itself be Nation-wide and world-wide. . . .

It is not possible by enactment of a law to make old drinkers stop drinking, to change the deep-seated habits of a lifetime. The amendment proposed in this resolution does not undertake to coerce old drinkers or to regulate the use of liquor by the individual.

The cure for this disease lies in the stopping of the debauching of the young. Our generation must establish such conditions that hereafter the young will grow up sober. This proposed amendment is scientifically drawn to attain this end.

Members of the Women's Christian Temperance Union (WCTU), an organization concerned about the destructive power of alcohol, march in Washington D.C. in 1909 to present a petition supporting prohibition. Topical Press Agency/Hulton Getty Archive/Getty Images.

Upon this all must agree. A man may drink himself, but if he is a good man he would love to see such conditions established that the young hereafter would grow up sober. . . .

I have known many drinkers, but I have never yet known one who made a habit of teaching boys to drink. This sinister agent is the Liquor Trust of America.

Teaching the Young to Drink

Tens of thousands of paid agents all over the land are carrying out this devilish work. The most deadly work thus far has been in the cities where it is hard for parents to keep track of their boys, but it extends to towns and is now being systematically extended to country settlements. The usual method in cities is to operate where boys come together, sometimes having the boys rendevous [sic] in saloons but more frequently in pool rooms and other places of amusement, sometimes on vacant lots. The bootlegger or licensed agent of the Liquor Trust arranges to have the boys drink before breaking up to be sociable or as a sign of manliness. . . .

The real motive in teaching the boys to drink is to develop future customers. With a reasonably small outlay the Liquor Trust can develop this appetite in the young and when the young grow up with an appetite then as men they buy the liquor, over the supply of which the Liquor Trust has a monopoly. The large profits in the sale of their goods to customers thus developed is the real motive of the great Liquor Trust in systematically debauching the youth of the Nation.

The real scientific way to cure this evil therefore is to remove the motive—the profits in the sale of the goods. Clearly, this can not be done by undertaking to coerce those who drink, but it can be done by prohibiting the sale and everything that relates to the sale, particularly to the manufacture for sale. This can be done the more readily as barter and sale for profit have been subject to public control since the earliest days.

When the motive is removed and the liquor interests can no longer derive profits from the sale, then the great Liquor Trust of necessity will disintegrate. The debauching of the young will thus end and the young generation will grow up sober.

In this way no effort is made to coerce any citizen. Some old drinkers desiring to stop will take advantage of the changed environment and stop, and other old drinkers desiring to do so will continue drinking until they die, subject to local or State regulation or control; but when they die no new drinkers will take their place and the next generation will be sober. This method thus takes no chance of invading the sanctity of the home or the liberties of the individual. Some men may feel that they have an inherent right to drink liquor, but no man will feel that he has a right to sell liquor. . . .

Local or National?

In carrying out the prohibition of the sale, manufacture for sale, and all that relates to sale, the next question that arises is whether the scope of the prohibition should be limited to small units, like the town and the county, or should extend to the large units making it State wide and nation wide. It is good to have a town dry rather than wet. It is better to have a county dry rather than wet; but if prohibition is by the small unit, then wet towns and wet counties will be found near by, and the virus there generated will pass over continuously and reinfect the dry town and the dry county. It is a good thing to cut out one root of a cancer, it is a better thing to cut out another root, but as long as a single root remains it will generate the virus and inject it into the circulation and reinfect the whole system. As long as there is one State in the Union that is wet it will be the base of operations and source of supply for the national Liquor Trust, from which, through interstate commerce, to infect all the other States. Poison generated in any part of the body, projected into the circulation, will reach all parts of the body, and no part can protect itself. The States can not protect themselves against interstate commerce, nor can Congress delegate to the States this power. The liquor traffic is the most interstate of all business. Their organization is a national organization. It is dealt with by the National Government.

Under our present system limiting prohibition to small units, the great Liquor Trust has trampled upon the rights of States, of counties, and of towns, and has taken pride in proclaiming that "prohibition does not prohibit."

This pose of the liquor outlaw that he is above the operations of local law is a complete and conclusive demonstration of the need of a national law. There can be no cure of a cancer until all the roots have been cut out, until no centers of contagion are left to reinfect. Local option in various forms, and even State-wide prohibition, though valuable and useful, have not proved adequate. Our whole experience shows that *prohibition must be national.*

If Congress, in the exercise of the taxing power, should undertake to establish prohibition by statute, the great Liquor Trust would not permanently disintegrate, because what any one Congress can do another Congress can undo. Wet and dry elections would be continually following each other all the time, and the country would be wet part of the time and dry part of the time, and the youth would not have time to grow up sober—the remedy would only be superficial.

To cure this organic disease we must have recourse to the organic law [the fundamental law of the United States, the Constitution]. The people themselves must act upon this question. A generation must be prevailed upon to place prohibition in their own constitutional law, and such a generation could be counted upon to keep it in the Constitution during its lifetime. The Liquor Trust of necessity would disintegrate. The youth would grow up sober. The final, scientific conclusion is that we must have constitutional prohibition, prohibiting only the sale, the manufacture for sale, and everything that pertains to the sale, and invoke the power of both Federal and State Governments for enforcement. The resolution is drawn to fill these requirements.

The Power of Truth

If you ask me how to cause the people of a generation to take the question into their own hands and act. I answer without hesitation, reach them with the truth about alcohol. Thorough education in this appalling truth, if it comes not too late in life, will cause the individual to adopt total abstinence and the people to destroy the traffic root and branch. The liquor interests realize this fact full well. They spend millions every year in their efforts to control the liquor policies of the press and keep the truth about alcohol from the people. They try to destroy any man who dares to undertake this work. After my first investigations as to the truth about alcohol I introduced the results of my labors and put them in the CONGRESSIONAL RECORD in a speech called the Great Destroyer and proceeded to send this speech systematically to the youth of America. I estimate that I have sent out about 2,500,000 copies and have sent out more than a million and a half individual letters to the youth on this subject. It is this work that has brought down the arm of the great liquor interests in their efforts to destroy me politically.

In the recent senatorial primary in Alabama it was not simply my distinguished and powerful opponent, but the great liquor interests of the Nation that I had to fight. . . . Of course I was defeated and my fate was held up as a warning to other men in public life. Perhaps I might add what I said in a card to the papers of Alabama the day after the primary, to notify the liquor interests of America that I had simply finished my training, and that I had only begun to fight, and that I would meet them on a hundred battle fields and they would find me in the thick of the fight when the thirty-sixth State ratifies the resolution, which may perhaps go down in history under the name of the Hobson resolution, that will put prohibition into the Constitution of the United States forever. . . .

[The liquor interests] talk of minorities dictating to majorities. As a matter of fact, they can not find any practical conditions where a majority of the people of the United States to-day would be found against national prohibition. A substantial majority of our people to-day are living under prohibition law. They do not seem willing to let three-fourths of the States decide upon the organic question, but would rather have one-fourth of the States insist upon allowing the country to remain wet. . . .

Liquor really has no case in the light of discoveries of science giving us the truth about alcohol.

The further continuance of the liquor traffic is absolutely indefensible. The forces of society are now gathering throughout the whole world. The battle line is drawn. Some might wish that the battle be deferred for their own reasons, but the war is now on, the first battle is now in progress. I want all members to bear in mind when they cast their vote what this great war means. When our country is sober and degeneracy no longer lowers the standard of character of humanity it will then be possible to solve the problems of the Nation which are now so acute on account of degeneracy, social, economic, and moral problems. It will permit the rapid advance of humanity to the point where it will be possible to have universal peace, hastening the day when liberty and free institutions will be universal and when man will cooperate in a great brotherhood of man under the fatherhood of God.

Some of my colleagues are not to return to the Sixty-fourth Congress, like myself; others are to remain here. To both alike I make my appeal. I know there is danger in confronting this great and powerful enemy, but in time of war the good soldier does not stop because of danger. I do not ask you to go where I would not go myself. It may be that I am politically dead, my political life destroyed by the liquor interest, but I do not hesitate to say that I am not afraid of political death. I would rather hold my hand up and fight like a man though I had to die a hundred political deaths. I would rather to-day do a man's part in this struggle to cut the millstone of degeneracy from the neck of humanity—I would rather do that than to be United States Senator from Alabama, and if I know my own mind I would rather do that than be President of the United States. I call on you, my colleagues, to hold your heads up in the face of this enemy and be men. In the name of your manhood, in the name of your patriotism, in the name of all that is held dear by good men, in the name of your fireside, in the name of our institutions, in the name of our country, in the name of humanity and of humanity's God, I call on you to join hands with me and each one to do his full duty.

The Eighteenth Amendment Will Not Harm Workers and Should Be Submitted for Ratification

William Jennings Bryan

William Jennings Bryan was a prominent lawyer and one of the most popular speakers of the early twentieth century. He was the Democratic nominee for president of the United States in the elections of 1896, 1900, and 1908 and later became the U.S. secretary of state. He was a strong advocate of Prohibition and his campaigning helped to pass the Eighteenth Amendment. The following open letter to the chairman of the Judiciary Committee of the House of Representatives was published in the Washington Post *on December 17, 1917, the day the House passed the resolution calling for the amendment. A full-page paid political advertisement, it was Bryan's response to a letter published the previous day in the* Washington Star *by union leader Samuel Gompers, the founder of the American Federation of Labor. In his response Bryan argues against Gompers's proposal to postpone the submission of the amendment for ratification, disagreeing with the suggestion that it would be unfair to workers who might lose their jobs or that it would detract from unity during the war (World War I, then in progress). In Bryan's opinion, however, wage earners would benefit from the banishment of saloons.*

I have just read in *The Sunday Star* Mr. [Samuel] Gompers' appeal to Congress to postpone the submission of the Constitutional amendment prohibiting the manufacture and sale of intoxicating liquors.

William Jennings Bryan, "An Open Letter to Hon. Edwin Y. Webb, Chairman, Judiciary Committee of the House of Representatives, on the Pending National Prohibition Amendment," paid political advertisement, *Washington Post*, December 17, 1917.

I beg to call your attention to certain implications contained in his open letter which convert his appeal into a strong argument in favor of immediate submission of the amendment:

First: By singling out the nine subordinate organizations for which he speaks, namely, the United Brotherhood of Carpenters and Joiners, United Brewery Workers' Union, Cigarmakers' International Union, Glass Bottle Blowers' Union, International Coopers' Union, International Union of Steam and Operating Engineers, Brotherhood of Stationary Firemen, American Federation of Musicians, and Hotel and Restaurant Employees and Bartenders' International Alliance, he admits that the Federation of Labor, as a whole, does not support him in the position which he takes. In fact, he expressly disclaims that he speaks officially when he says:

"I do not address you and through you the Judiciary Committee as an officer of any organization, but as a man and a citizen," etc.

Few Workers Will Lose Their Jobs

And of the nine branches for which he assumes to speak, only two (which will be mentioned later) will suffer materially by the adoption of Prohibition and they only temporarily.

The Carpenters, for instance, cannot suffer, because more people can and will build homes, as is shown in the States that are dry. The Steam Engineers and Stationary Firemen cannot suffer because the money lost to liquor houses will give increased patronage to those engaged in other kinds of business. The Cigarmakers will not suffer because a decreasing percentage of the total output of cigars is handled by the saloons—already there are twenty-seven States in which prohibition has been adopted and several States will be added to the list next year [1918]. Coopers will not suffer because more barrels will be needed for food when less money is spent on drink, and, as for the Bottle Blowers, they will be kept busy

State	Ratified XVIII	Ratified XXI
Alabama	January 15, 1919	August 8, 1933
Arizona	May 24, 1918	September 5, 1933
Arkansas	January 14, 1919	August 1, 1933
California	January 13, 1919	July 24, 1933
Colorado	January 15, 1919	September 26, 1933
Connecticut	May 6, 1919	July 11, 1933
Delaware	March 18, 1918	June 24, 1933
Florida	December 3, 1918	November 14, 1933
Georigia	June 26, 1918	
Idaho	January 8, 1919	October 17, 1933
Illinois		July 10, 1933
Indiana		June 26, 1933
Iowa	January 15, 1919	July 10, 1933
Kansas	January 14, 1919	
Kentucky	January 14, 1918	November 27, 1933
Louisiana	August 3, 1918	
Maine	January 8, 1919	December 6, 1933
Maryland	February 13, 1918	October 18, 1933
Massachusetts	April 2, 1918	June 26, 1933
Michigan	January 2, 1919	April 10, 1933
Minnesota	January 17, 1919	October 10, 1933
Mississippi	January 8, 1918	
Missouri	January 16, 1919	August 29, 1933
Montana	February 19, 1918	August 6, 1934

[CONTINUED]

making bottles for milk for the babies that are now neglected and bottles for the soft drinks which are taking the place of intoxicating beverages.

Mr. Gompers speaks for only a *few* of the laboring men, for only a few can, by any possibility, lose employment because of the abolition of the saloons. Among the nine organizations mentioned there are, however, two whose members will be temporarily affected—the Brewery Workers and the Bartenders. They certainly will lose their jobs, but with the present demand for labor they will have no difficulty in finding employment which will pay them better than their present work and be more satisfactory to them and their families.

In his effort to aid a small fraction of the laboring men of the country, Mr. Gompers overlooks the material and moral

[CONTINUED]

State	Ratified XVIII	Ratified XXI
Nebraska	January 16, 1919	
Nevada	January 21, 1919	September 5, 1933
New Hampshire	January 15, 1919	July 11, 1933
New Jersey	March 9, 1922	June 1, 1933
New Mexico	January 20, 1919	November 2, 1933
New York	January 29, 1919	June 27, 1933
North Carolina	January 16, 1919	
North Dakota	January 25, 1918	
Ohio	January 7, 1919	December 5, 1933
Oklahoma	January 7, 1919	
Oregon	January 15, 1919	August 7, 1933
Pennsylvania	February 25, 1919	December 5, 1933
Rhode Island	(Rejected)	May 8, 1933
South Carolina	January 29, 1918	(Rejected)
South Dakota	March 20, 1918	
Tennessee	January 13, 1919	August 11, 1933
Texas	March 4, 1918	November 24, 1933
Utah	January 16, 1919	December 5, 1933
Vermont	January 29, 1919	September 23, 1933
Virginia	January 11, 1918	October 25, 1933
Washington	January 13, 1919	October 3, 1933
West Virginia	January 9, 1919	July 25, 1933
Wisconsin	January 17, 1919	April 25, 1933
Wyoming	January 16, 1919	May 25, 1933

welfare of a large majority of the wage earners who will be blessed by the banishment of drinking places. Would it not have been more fair for Mr. Gompers to have given both sides? Should he not have referred, for instance, to the Prohibition resolutions passed by the Locomotive Engineers, numbering 70,000? Why does he fail to mention the increasing support which laboring men are giving to Prohibition in State and nation?

No Right to Demand Saloons

Second: Mr. Gompers, by his silence, repudiates the "personal liberty" argument—the stock argument of the liquor interests for so many years. And well he may, for it is an outcast and an outlaw. The public is too well informed now as to the evils inseparably connected with the saloon, to tolerate any longer the impudent assertion that any man's "personal liberty" includes the right to demand the establishment of saloons which cannot exist without impairing the productive power of the community, ruining homes, impoverishing families, menacing morals, producing poverty, manufacturing criminals, debauching society and corrupting politics.

Third: Mr. Gompers' feeble plea for States' rights comes with poor grace from one who is defending a business which tramples roughshod on the rights of States as well as on the rights of smaller communities whenever they ask for a voice or a vote on any proposition connected with the saloons. In Texas the liquor interests have recently prevented the submission of a Prohibition amendment to the State constitution, and they did this in spite of the expressed wish of a Democratic primary and in spite of the fact that a large majority of the legislators in both houses favored submission. In New Jersey the liquor interests have fought bitterly against local option and tried to prevent legislation giving a vote even to cities and towns. Those who make a profit out of the liquor business do not respect the right of *any* community, large or small, to protect itself from the saloon. The reserved rights of the States are necessary to them and to the nation; we cannot afford to jeopardize these rights by linking them with the fate of the saloon—we cannot afford to chain them to a corpse.

Unity in Wartime

But Mr. Gompers' plea for postponement is, when analyzed, even a more convincing argument in favor of Prohibition. He says:

"A large number of Americans, whether natives or by adoption, drink beer, and in some instances light wines, as a part of their daily meals. Is prohibition or the threat of prohibition calculated to tranquillize and win them to the support of our country and the great cause in which we are engaged—or otherwise? Is it wise to bring so great a controversial question to the foreground during these crucial days when we need the united support, in spirit and action, of all our people?"

He exaggerates the number of those whose loyalty to Bacchus and Barleycorn and Gambrinus [mythical characters associated with wine and beer] is greater than their loyalty to their government. I am not willing to admit that the alcoholic habit is so firmly fixed in any large number of our people that their patriotism must be measured by the quart or that it depends upon the amount of intoxicating liquor which they can obtain. If we have any considerable number of such, then the very existence of this overmastering appetite is a menace to the nation; it makes the beer schooner more dangerous than the German submarine. We had better remove the alcoholic appendix than allow it to imperil its victims. This threat of disloyalty on the part of the liquor interests ought not to turn the people from their purpose to free the country from its greatest enemy. If the advocates of beer will not support the government with words unless the saloons are permitted to aid the enemy, we can better afford to lose their vocal support than tolerate their business.

Mr. Gompers cites the action of European nations on this question as if it were worthy of imitation, evidently forgetting that we have already refused to follow their example and made it unlawful to sell any kind of intoxicating liquor to a soldier in uniform. Shall we repeal that wholesome law in order to conform to European standards, or shall we continue to set them an example? Instead of patterning after the nations that feed alcohol to their soldiers, it is better to go even farther than we have and restrain those who would, by the manufacture and sale of liquor, sap the strengths of the men who must produce food and fashion the weapons of war.

Mr. Gompers pleads for unity, but how shall unity be obtained? By servile submission to a brewery autocracy whose methods are as unscrupulous as the methods of the Kaiser [the leader of Germany, against whom the United States and its allies were fighting in World War I]? No. Let unity be obtained by applying the fundamental democratic doctrine of acquiescence in the will of the majority.

Mr. Gompers has in the past done yeoman service in behalf of democracy; I feel sure that he will, on reflection, see that the best way to help win the war is to recognize the right of the people to rule in the United States as well as elsewhere, especially when the rights of the minority are so carefully safeguarded as to require the endorsement of the prohibition amendment by thirty-six of the forty-eight States before it can become a part of the Constitution of the United States. If the American people are not competent to sit in judgment on the question of saloons, with what consistency can they commend popular government to the people of any other country?

California Prohibitionists Should Focus Their Efforts on Ratification of the Eighteenth Amendment

Los Angeles Times

The following article is a news story from the Los Angeles Times *that appeared in February 1918, reporting on a convention of prohibitionists at which the delegates decided to work toward the election of state legislators pledged to vote for ratification of the Eighteenth Amendment. Great enthusiasm for nationwide prohibition was displayed at this convention, with delegates shouting for recognition and in some cases climbing on chairs. A minority argued for placing a "bone-dry" measure on the state ballot—many states at that time had already banned the sale of liquor—but the majority favored dropping that idea in order to focus on ratification. In the closing address, the speaker emphasized unity in support of the war effort (World War I was then in progress), and according to the reporter, "The war spirit was injected into the almost 1000 delegates." Like many of their era, they considered the winning of the war and the fight for Prohibition to be noble causes that were in some way associated, if only through the dedication of their supporters.*

Five hundred and twenty-five delegates, some of them excited, all of them in earnest—Prohibitionists, W.C.T.U. [Women's Christian Temperance Union] women, anti-saloon leaguers, Good Templars, "drys" from every county in California—this afternoon, by a vote of 355 to 170, decided to unite in a fight to elect Senators and Assemblymen who will be pledged to ratify the national prohibition amendment.

"California Anti-liquor Forces to War for Legislature Committed to National Amendment," *Los Angeles Times*, February 6, 1918.

For six hours lawyers, farmers, capitalists, ministers, laymen, bankers and merchants debated the two reports of the Continuation Committee of the California Campaign Federation.

The united "dry" forces decided against placing a "bone-dry" measure on the [California state] ballot at the election in November. It was determined also to unite behind a Governor and Lieutenant Governor who will agree to make the race on a "dry" platform.

From the moment when Chairman A.I. Wallace called California's largest "dry" convention to order, until the heated debate was closed with prayer by Rev. I. Clarence Pinkerton, delegations fought for a unity which came in a sensational climax as the vote was tabulated.

Two leaders easily were granted the honors by the opposing sides. D.M. Gandler, State superintendent of the Anti-Saloon League, was standard bearer for the majority of the committee. He urged a fight for a Legislature that will ratify the national prohibition amendment.

Herbert A. Wheeler, also of Los Angeles, became standard bearer for the minority members of the committee. Each side arranged its forces and the leaders were each granted fifteen minutes and the speakers five minutes each to present the arguments in favor of the two propositions.

The majority members, under Gandler's leadership, favored a legislative fight only. The minority members, under Wheeler, wanted a "bone-dry" amendment to the Constitution of the State of California. . . .

Liquor Traffic Doomed

As the tide of battle surged, delegates shouted for recognition. Some climbed upon chairs, others waved arms frantically. There was a tense feeling as the champions were chosen. Seasoned warriors who have been in the van of the "drys" many years came to the platform and the large crowd on the floor

An 1888 lithograph titled Principles of the Prohibition Party, *contains images of then-presidential candidate Clinton Bowen Fisk, and his running mate, John A. Brooks. Bettmann/Corbis.*

of the auditorium and in the galleries was swayed to tears and then to cheers as the speakers pleaded their side of the case.

Faint praise for the Rominger bill [a California state bill abolishing saloons and regulating the sale of alcohol] was silenced by fierce invectives. One speaker wanted the ordinance "relegated to hell" and called it "junk." Orators attacked it and early in the afternoon it was seen that an indorsement for the bill was impossible. . . .

When the boards were cleared for action at the afternoon session Chairman Wallace gave Gandler the platform. The convention had sung "America." The delegates were prepared to do their level best. There was the usual attempt of many to confuse the chair. The former Lieutenant Governor refused to be stampeded. He gave the "dry" champion the rostrum, and the superintendent of the Anti-Saloon League was never in finer form.

There was a hush of expectancy, the great crowd waited. It wanted to applaud and Gandler, as he stepped forward, was given an ovation such as few speakers on a dry [antialcohol] subject have ever received. With carefully chosen words he opened the argument for a legislative fight as he said:

"Wise decisions made today are not for California only, but for the United States and for the world. There is no question, in my mind, but that the liquor traffic is doomed. We all want absolute prohibition as soon as possible. Thank God, it's a question of method as to how we shall get it and after the majority has spoken we will abide by the result.

"We have at least thirty-two states that will ratify the Congressional amendment. There are two that are doubtful, we must get two others and make it thirty-six. Now if California will ratify the amendment next January the entire country will ratify before January, 1920."

When Gandler closed the convention, delegates and the galleries broke forth and the applause lasted five minutes. California had practically decided against a bone-dry State fight.

H.A. Wheeler, leader of the minority, looked nervous as he took the floor. It was seen that he had a fairly strong following, but he fought a losing fight. . . .

Tense Excitement

"If the delegates will step down or climb down from their seats, the discussion will continue," said Chairman Wallace, as he saw how tense was the excitement. Then the chairman selected speakers for the closing minutes of the contest. . . .

A.M. Drew of Fresno declared the people of Los Angeles are so good they don't want to go to heaven and said the people of San Francisco are so bad they'd be out of place in hell.

Mrs. Marie G. Brehm of Long Beach talked too long and when called down by the chairman she declared that she will run for the Legislature this year.

Dr. James A. Geissinger, one of the leaders of the opposition, said: "You may call us extremists, radicals or any name you like, but there are hundreds of thousands of people who want to vote on a bone-dry measure.

"I'm an abolitionist. I voted for Woodrow Wilson, and I thank God I did."

As the President's name was mentioned, there was round after round of applause. . . .

That the war [World War I] might be pressed to a successful conclusion and that President Wilson might be assured of the united support of the delegates of the Fresno dry convention was the wish expressed by Rev. Josiah Sibley, pastor of Calvary Presbyterian Church, in the closing address.

The speaker lauded the "gallant army of Belgium, the veterans of France, the Tommies [soldiers] of England" and declared that the Sammies [a nickname for U.S. soldiers] will go over the top after the Germans have wasted themselves in the great spring drive, certain that the entire nation is back of them.

The war spirit was injected into the almost 1000 delegates as the speaker urged cooperation in the plan to make California one of the thirty-six States that will make the United States bone dry.

"It will be my proud boast," said Chairman Wallace, "to be able to say I presided over the great convention in 1918 that made California dry. This is a wonderful day and a glorious finish to a great work. Now let us see to it that we are on duty every minute until this great task is accomplished."

Prohibition Will End Political Corruption in America

Robert B. Armstrong

Robert B. Armstrong was assistant secretary of the treasury under President Theodore Roosevelt and publicity manager for the presidential campaigns of Warren G. Harding, Calvin Coolidge, and Herbert Hoover. He was a correspondent for the Los Angeles Times *and in 1922 was president of the National Press Club. In the following article he wrote for the* Times *on the day the Eighteenth Amendment was ratified, he speculates that Prohibition will bring about political reform in America. He points out that the notoriously corrupt politicians who at that time controlled large cities such as New York and Chicago were closely involved with the liquor trade and that some of them were saloon keepers. Armstrong expresses a belief that municipal and state government will be immensely improved by the elimination of saloons and that the destructive forces resulting from legalized liquor traffic "will be forever banished." He, like most Americans, failed to foresee that illegal liquor traffic would bring about even worse corruption.*

Momentous as the moral, industrial and economic results sure to follow the adoption of a nation-wide, permanent prohibition amendment to the Federal Constitution, made certain today by Nebraska's action, they are likely to be overshadowed during the first years of its application by the revolutionary political effect of the abolition of "booze."

In New York, Chicago, Cleveland, Boston, San Francisco and scores of smaller cities the Democratic local organization has been built and for years maintained on a booze basis.

Robert B. Armstrong, "Saloons' Political Grip on Country Is Broken," *Los Angeles Times*, January 17, 1919.

Similarly, in Philadelphia, Cincinnati, Pittsburgh, Milwaukee and many other cities, the saloon and the liquor traffic have been the backbone of Republican strength.

With nation-wide, bone-dry prohibition in effect next January 16, 1920, saloons everywhere abolished and the liquor business in every form outlawed, the 1920 Presidential campaign, with the collateral State and municipal campaigns, will be conducted along radically revised lines.

Tammany Hall Weakened

In New York it has been the strangle hold which it had on the saloon-keepers, the brewers and the distillery owners which has preserved intact the notorious Tammany organization [a political machine that controlled New York in the late nineteenth and early twentieth centuries] despite years of adversity and defeat. The corner saloon has been the headquarters for the Tammany precinct captains, ward heelers and neighborhood gang leaders. It paid regularly its tribute in cash to the Tammany chief and in return was assured his protection.

Can Tammany survive with its source of revenue cut off? Tammany never was more powerful or arrogant than it is today with a Tammany Mayor in the City Hall, Tammany Governor at Albany and the Tammany organization constantly nourished by patronage favors from the Democratic administration at Washington. Tammany may be able to outlive the saloon, but it will certainly not be the same Tammany; there will be fewer dark stripes.

Likewise, in Chicago, in a lesser degree, the banishment of booze will threaten the reign of "Bathhouse John" Coughlin and "Hinky Dink" Kenna, for decades political czars of that city's Tenderloin wards [area of a city devoted to vice] who exert a malevolent influence over the government of the entire city.

A New York City liquor store advertisement from 1919 urges customers to stock up before national Prohibition goes into effect. It reads, "Buy Now! This is the time to acquire your liquors."

Saloon-Owning Political Chiefs

"Bathhouse John" and "Hinky Dink" are themselves saloon-keepers and hold their power solely by virtue of the personal control they exercise over liquor traffic in their respective bailiwicks. Moreover they are the dominating force in the Democratic organization of Chicago and their decrees are heard and respected in the councils of the State organization.

In Cleveland the liquor interests for years have supported and financed the Democratic organization in both city and county and have often dictated its policies and candidates. Even during the purified Baker regime, the saloons and breweries supplied the bone and sinew and much of the brains.

The late "Boss" George B. Cox was himself a saloon-keeper and constructed his great Cincinnati organization on the saloon basis. When he rose to power in State politics he had at his command unlimited funds supplied by the millionaire Cincinnati brewers and distillers and the Hamilton county Republican organization is even now held together and made powerful by the same interests as strikingly evidenced by the late November election.

Political Reform

The same story may be told and retold a hundred times in the political history of American municipalities. That the passing of the saloon and the legalized liquor traffic and the coming of prohibition gives assurance of a mighty political reformation is affirmed by national dry leaders and this is not denied by the vanquished wets.

That the standard of municipal and State government will be immensely improved would seem likely. The root of graft and inefficiency which have flourished and given America the name of being the worst governed country, locally, in the world will have been killed and the multitude of noxious, degenerating and destructive forces which can be traced directly to the saloon will be forever banished.

What the effect will be with regard to the Presidential election next year [1920] is difficult to estimate. It is true, however, that the liquor traffic was much more of an asset to the Democrats than to the Republicans and the Democratic party will suffer the largest measure of financial and organization distress by its prospective elimination.

The Prohibition Law Is Discriminatory and Hypocritical

W.H. Stayton

W.H. Stayton, a former naval officer, was the founder of the Association Against the Prohibition Amendment. In the following article he argues that Prohibition can never be enforced because it does not command the respect of the public. It is a discriminatory law, he says, because the poor have been denied beer, their favorite beverage, while the rich continue to drink liquor they can afford to obtain illegally. The more enforcement agents and arrests there are, the greater the number of violations, and in his opinion this is due to the fact that those who passed the law are hypocritical. He states that many, including federal officials, do not even pretend to obey it; they view it merely as something that benefits the lower class. This is not democracy, Stayton says, and people will continue to be resentful—in a free country, he argues, lawmaking bodies should enact only measures that are reasonable and have public support.

The prohibition law will never be enforced.

Try as we may to believe that the American people are law-abiding and staunch supporters of the laws on our statute books, we cannot but arrive at one conclusion, viz: that the national prohibition law is discriminatory class legislation. In practice it has been found to operate unequally. The rich continue to drink, but the poor have been denied their favorite beverage—a wholesome beer of low alcoholic content. Such a law can never be enforced because it can never command popular respect. Furthermore, prohibitory legislation enacted at the behest of a minority will always be held in contempt and disrespect by the majority.

W.H. Stayton, "Is National Prohibition a Success?" con, *Congressional Digest*, October 1924.

We may today carry out the suggestion of Mr. Henry Ford (who recently announced that he would discharge any employee presenting himself for work with liquor on his breath) that the Army, Navy and Marine Corps be employed to carry out the provisions of the Volstead Act [the actual law that prohibited the manufacture and sale of alcohol by authority of the Eighteenth Amendment], and yet, judging by the nation's experience over the past four years, we will have wholesale violations and heavier tax burdens to meet. We may even enact into law the Cramton bill clothing the 1,000 Washington policemen with powers of Federal enforcement agents, and the violations instead of being lessened, will increase, if the past is any criterion.

Violations Increase

It is generally true that the larger the number of government, State and local officers engaged in attempted prohibition enforcement, the more arrests; but, it must be remembered that increased arrests tend to show conclusively the unpopularity of the law and the consequent impossibility of its enforcement. Our jails and prisons have been crowded to capacity for the last four years with persons who have failed to obey a law, in the framing of which they had no hand. Instead of this being a lesson to other persons, violations have steadily increased until, today, reports made by the various branches of the enforcement unit show that more people violate the law than ever before.

Each year, Prohibition Commissioner [Roy] Haynes has asked Congress for large appropriations to enforce the Volstead Law. Each year these estimates have far exceeded those of the previous year and now the Budget Bureau is considering the request of Mr. Haynes for an appropriation slightly in excess of $25,000,000, a small portion of which would be used for prohibition enforcement by the United States Coast Guard. Large amounts have been spent in equipping and operating a "rum fleet" of revenue cutters to prevent liquor-laden ships from reaching the United States and landing their cargoes. But violations of the law have increased with the increased vigilance of the Federal Government.

Law Passed by Hypocrites

One of the important factors in bringing about the present state of contempt for and disobedience to the Volstead Law is found in the public's knowledge that those who drew the law and voted for its passage do not even pretend to obey it. People with ideas of liberty are not inclined to obey laws confessedly hypocritical and concededly passed by hypocrites. Indeed, the student of government will find in this instance something graver than even hypocrisy. For our federal officials, even those in very high places, do not hesitate to say, in effect, "Yes, I disregard the Volstead Act, for I am a gentleman and an educated man and I know how to drink and when to stop. The law was not intended for such as we are, but for the other class of our people, and it is for their good to have it." No man knows what may happen in a Republic when those who make, administer and execute the laws have come to think of "their people" much as they do of "their cattle." Certainly this is not democracy, and certainly the "cattle" are going to continue their resentfulness and work for a change.

Prohibitionists cry out that the people are wrong and should obey the law. The people answer that it is the law which is wrong, and that it should be changed.

Why this law should be held in such contempt by the people who are otherwise law-abiding is still a matter of controversy. Some condemn it for one reason, some for another. A leading New England newspaper sees in the public's attitude a warning that we should "begin a serious study of all laws which do not command public favor" because in a Republic "a law which does not command public support is not a law—it is a form of tyranny."

One who studies the psychology of the subject is inevitably struck by the anomaly that while State prohibition laws are generally obeyed and respected, people seem to feel it a sort of duty to flout the Volstead Act. And inquiry quickly reveals at least one reason—a belief that the law was passed not by a man's neighbors, who had an interest in him and his affairs, but by someone living at a distance, by strangers acting in a spirit of meddle-someness.

No good can come from merely berating the public because a law is disobeyed. There are two sides to the subject. Undoubtedly, there is an obligation on all of us to obey the law, but in a free country there is a corresponding obligation on the part of the lawmaking bodies to enact only such measures as are fair and reasonable and will command the support of public opinion. Those lawmakers who foisted national prohibition upon us committed the first and the great wrong, and upon them rests the responsibility for our present lawlessness.

The Volstead Act Should Be Modified to Allow Beer and Wine

Walter E. Edge

Walter E. Edge was a U.S. senator representing New Jersey from 1919 to 1929. Before that and again later on he was that state's governor. The following statement is a portion of his testimony at a hearing before the U.S. Senate Committee on the Judiciary in April 1926. In it he advocates modifying the law to permit beer and light wine, which he believes will enable the prohibition of stronger drink to be enforced. In his opinion this would be constitutional because whereas the Eighteenth Amendment prohibits intoxicating liquors, the amount of alcohol deemed to be intoxicating is a matter for Congress to decide. The Volstead Act was what set the percentage so low that beer could not be sold, and as a result people turned to the hard liquor available from bootleggers, whose trade, he argues, would be greatly reduced if beer were legal. In answer to the claim this would bring back saloons (establishments where liquor is sold by the drink), Edge says that he has not heard of any proposals to legalize them and that public opinion will never again permit it, whether or not the law allows them. This prediction proved to be wrong—when Prohibition was repealed such establishments immediately returned under the new name of bars, taverns or cocktail lounges, albeit with a better atmosphere than they had had before being patronized by women.

I will not take the time of the committee with the presentation of either evidence or statistics for the purpose of establishing the appalling failure of prohibition. Senator [William Cable] Bruce has well covered that situation.

Walter E. Edge, testimony before the U.S. Senate Committee on the Judiciary, April 1926.

In my judgment, and I am quite sure in the judgment of a large majority of the people of this country, prohibition has not only failed to prohibit but has created an atmosphere of protest and challenge, an almost defiance which demands congressional consideration.

Of course, no one defends violation of the law, no matter how unjust a law may be, but it avails us nothing to fall back on the defense that the law should and must be enforced. All law should be, but the facts are it is not enforced, and in my judgment, never can be satisfactorily enforced.

Neither is this a plea to relieve a situation simply because citizens refuse to abide by the law, but if it can be demonstrated and it can, that the law is unfair and is an unjust interpretation of the Constitution, then it is our duty to recognize such a situation.

Any law that brings in its wake such wide corruption in the public service, increased alcoholic insanity, and deaths, increased arrests for drunkenness, home barrooms, and development among young boys and young women of the use of the flask never heard of before prohibition can not be successfully defended.

My purpose in addressing the committee is to endeavor to offer constructive suggestions which I believe will improve conditions. Certainly, they could not be worse than they are to-day.

Those who urge modification of the Volstead Act are usually classified as encouraging violation of the law. What a travesty! No more ridiculous assertion could be made.

I unhesitatingly contend that those who recognize existing evils and sincerely endeavor to correct them are contributing more toward temperance than those who stubbornly refuse to admit the facts. Some of us are enlisted in this movement in the interest of tolerance and temperance, and all the misrepresentations that can be made will not deter us from our purpose and determination.

Real Temperance

This is not a campaign to bring back intoxicating liquor, as is so often claimed by the fanatical dry. Intoxicating liquor is with us to-day and practically as accessible as it ever was. The difference mainly because of its illegality, is its greater destructive power, as evidenced on every hand. The sincere advocates of prohibition welcome efforts for real temperance rather than a continuation of the present bluff.

No sane man would support legislation which he believed would make conditions worse. I can not imagine such a citizen. In fact, it is difficult to believe they could be much worse than they are to-day.

Frequently we see the statement from the opposition that a modification of the Volstead Act will mark a return to the conditions prevailing before prohibition. With the saloons eliminated, the conditions before prohibition were infinitely better than to-day, and I have not heard of any legislation proposing to legalize saloons. We now have all the evils of preprohibition days plus many other evils we never imagined possible in the old days.

I confidently assert that if the Volstead Act is modified up to the point of constitutional limitation, as is universally demanded, much of the existing spirit of challenge and protest will be eliminated and violation of the law substantially reduced.

The time has arrived for Congress to cease trying to find excuses to postpone modification or to refuse to meet this situation. The time has arrived for Congress to help find a legal way to do so.

The opposition always proceeds on the theory that give them time and they will stop the habit of indulging in intoxicating beverages. This can not be accomplished. We should recognize our problem is not to persist in the impossible, but to recognize a situation and bring about common-sense temperance through reason.

I have introduced several bills proposing modification of the Volstead Act. Since introducing those bills, I have proposed several amendments to which I will later refer.

S. 33, introduced by me, provides for the increase of the maximum of alcohol permitted in beverages from the existing under one-half of 1 per cent to 2.75 per cent. I will not take the time of the committee to discuss this bill because since introducing it I have presented another bill which, in my judgment, better meets constitutional requirements that I fully recognize we must wrestle with.

Of course, any stated percentage as high as 2.75 per cent presents the familiar question of what is or is not intoxicating. Scientific witnesses take positive positions on both sides of this question. If such an amendment became a law no man can speak with definite knowledge as to the final decision of the Supreme Court.

Allowable Percentage of Alcohol

Opinions heretofore handed down by the Supreme Court clearly indicate the question of percentage is a matter for Congress to decide, and when the Volstead Act with its under one-half of 1 per cent limitation was upheld by the Supreme Court there was nothing to indicate the court would not have likewise upheld it if the percentage had been much higher.

In this connection I desire to refer to the original report which accompanied the Volstead Act when presented in the House of Representatives by its sponsor, Mr. Volstead, away back in 1919. Apparently there was absolutely no question in the minds of the majority of the Judiciary Committee of the House at that time as to the power of Congress to fix the alcoholic limit as they deemed wise. . . .

As I have already indicated and as the committee are aware, I have sponsored another bill which, in my judgment, entirely removes any possible question of constitutionality.

S. 3118, introduced by me and referring to alcoholic contents, amends the Volstead Act by substituting the words "nonintoxicating in fact" for the present limitation of under one-half of 1 per cent. In other words, it copies and asserts the very words of the Constitution itself and its constitutionality therefore can not be questioned.

In connection with the introduction of this bill, I must go back a short period.

When the Volstead Act finally passed Congress and, upon the insistence primarily of representatives of the rural communities, section 29 was included in the act, a portion of which I will read.

> The penalties provided in this act against the manufacture of liquor without a permit shall not apply to a person for manufacturing nonintoxicating cider and fruit juices exclusively for use in his home, but such cider and fruit juices shall not be sold or delivered except to persons having permits to manufacture vinegar.

Under those provisions it is, of course, clearly established that citizens could produce nonintoxicating cider and fruit juices in their homes for home consumption.

For a long time after the passage of the act the question as to the alcoholic percentage permitted under this section was under dispute. The Government took the position that the general definition of intoxicating liquors in the act of one-half of 1 per cent or over likewise applied to section 29 and that cider or fruit juices thus produced would be illegal if they contained one-half of 1 per cent alcohol or more.

Various test cases as to this contention reached the Federal courts. The case of Congressman [John Philip] Hill, of Baltimore, where he had produced in his home ciders or fruit juices or wine to an admitted strength of over one-half of 1 per cent was tried in the Federal court and the Congressman acquitted of any violation of the Volstead Act. Other cases have been tried in Federal courts with like result.

One of these cases was recently appealed to the Federal court of appeals in the West Virginia district, the Eisner case, and the court of appeals sustained the lower court to the effect that fruit juices and ciders could be produced under section 29 up to the point of being "intoxicating in fact" and that any violation must be established by the complainant. . . .

Present Law Discriminatory

Perhaps I might interpolate here that intoxication in this section of the law means what you and I ordinarily understand as average human beings by the word "drunkenness." If this wine was capable of producing drunkenness when taken in sufficient quantities—that is to say, taken in such quantities as it was practically possible for a man to drink—then it was intoxicating.

Remember now, malt and cereal beverages, in other words, beers and ales are under the Volstead Act still violations of the law if they contain only one-half of 1 per cent alcohol, and many convictions have been secured under that provision.

No one can possibly or successfully defend such a glaring discrimination.

The farmer with his grapes or apples can legally go the limit. The industrial worker with his beer can go to jail.

This bill, S. 3118, has been introduced to remedy this situation. As stated, it simply substitutes the term "nonintoxicating in fact" for the term "one half of 1 per cent." It removes the present indefensible discrimination.

The effect of this bill if it became a law would legalize the manufacture, sale, and use of all beverages whether wine, cider, cereal, or malt to the point of being intoxicating in fact.

I have presented an amendment to the bill which prohibits the drinking of any such beverages in any place where sold. This is for the obvious purpose of preventing a return of the old-time legalized saloon. . . .

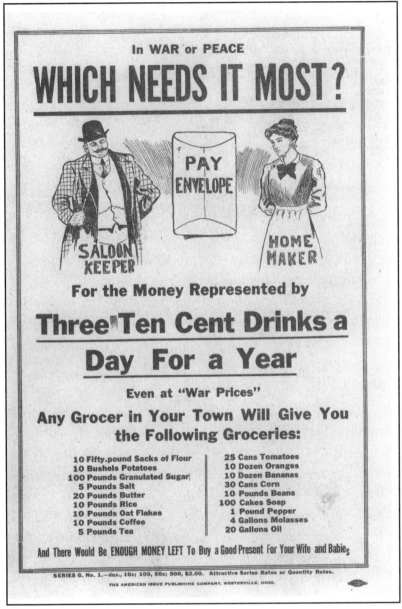

A poster, created between 1917 and 1918, shows a list of groceries that could be purchased with money used for drinks. The poster reads, "In War or Peace Which Needs It Most?" The National Prohibition Act (or Volstead Act) was passed a few years after this poster was published. Library of Congress.

I clearly realize when the other side takes the stand they will oppose modification as they have always done, mainly on three major counts:

1. That any modification is unconstitutional.
2. That even if it were not, the return of light wines and beers, so called, would not satisfy those who want hard spirits.
3. That legalizing their manufacture would mean the return of the saloons.

As to the constitutionality, as I have said, there is absolutely nothing to discuss. The very words used in the bill are the words of the Constitution. The Constitution prohibits intoxicating liquors. This bill likewise prohibits intoxicating liquors. If this bill is unconstitutional, then the eighteenth amendment itself is unconstitutional, which, of course, would be a ridiculous assertion. . . .

Saloons Will Never Return

This country was not a whisky-consuming country before prohibition. This contention is borne out by statements of representatives of the Anti-Saloon League itself. Senator [Clarence] Dill, of Washington, in a radio speech made in February [1926] stated "92 per cent of saloon business in the United States before prohibition was beer business." This same admission has been made by many other accredited representatives of the drys. . . . This, of course, is direct evidence that our citizens largely preferred malt and cereal beverages. These people to-day are not able to obtain such beverages with a percentage of one-half of 1 per cent or over without becoming criminals while much stronger wine and cider are legalized. The natural result is, of course, a great reduction in this consumption and a corresponding increase in drinking illicit synthetic gin and other poisonous concoctions.

Therefore it must be obvious to legalize light wine and beer to constitutional limits would greatly decrease the bootleggers' trade, and that is one of the reasons all efforts for modification are being opposed by the bootleggers' fraternity. Surely this is an accomplishment in the interest of temperance. The Antisaloon League, in the stubborn position they assume, are aiding the prosperity of this industry.

The claim that it would bring back saloons is, of course, advanced along to weaken modification. Legal saloons will never return to this country, whether the law prohibits them or otherwise. Public opinion would never permit it.

Prohibition Is a Modern Necessity and an Economic Success

Franklin W. Fort

Franklin W. Fort, an attorney, was a U.S. representative from New Jersey from 1925 to 1931. In the following article he argues that Prohibition resulted from the development of new technologies incompatible with drunkenness and from changes in social ethics, including women's suffrage, and that it has had economic benefits. High-speed machinery and factories with production lines could not function if some workers were impaired or absent due to drinking. Also, he says, the replacement of horses by automobiles meant that drivers had to be sober. In addition to this trend, the liberation of women, new laws protecting families, and the development of life insurance required men to be more responsible than when the male head of the house ruled arbitrarily. Fort maintains that the economic prosperity of the 1920s depended on Prohibition and that the manufacturers, bankers, and foreign representatives of his acquaintance all agreed on this. In his opinion, too much was made of the nonenforcement situation, as crime associated with illicit liquor existed before nationwide prohibition and was not new.

Major movements in human life come in great waves, and when one is in their midst he can see only the white-caps which dot the surface. To me it is entirely clear now that the agitation [for prohibition of alcohol] did not reach its powerful sweep through its own internal strength, did not lift itself by its own bootstraps, but was created by two irresistible ground swells in our national life for which it was but the channel.

Franklin W. Fort, "Shall the Eighteenth Amendment Stand?" *Congressional Digest*, March 1930.

One of these was the growing trend toward the mechanization of our whole life and the systematizing of our industry. With high-speed machinery and increased specialization in its use, alertness of mind and body became essential for both the safety of the worker and the efficiency of his work. With factories organized so that processes were continuous and a break at any point in the handling chain slowed all the wheels and hampered all the work, each workman's presence and correct performance must be assured. Midday drinking by one man might cause some cog to slip and injure either his fellow workman or the whole system. So, too, the plant must be fully manned every day, each specialized workman at his appointed task. No longer could our industries proceed with 50 per cent attendance Monday, 80 per cent Tuesday and 100 per cent perhaps by Wednesday noon.

In the old days of one- or two-men shops, it had not been so serious. If necessary, the delinquent could work later when sober and make up for lost time. But 8-hour days and the dependence of one man's work upon the other's made that impossible. Nor could industry stand strikes. The competitive pace was too fast. Most strikes were caused by poverty—and poverty thrives on liquor.

Then, too, machines were fast replacing horses. Now a horse could get home with a drunken driver but a railroad train, a trolley car, or an automobile could not. So, somehow, we must try to keep our drivers cold sober. And, of course, the licensed drinking place, for its very livelihood, had to try to make them drink.

The swelling power of our new economic era, therefore, had to match its sword against the saloon.

New Social Ethics

But this was not the only major trend of our past 50 years as a Nation. Side by side with education and industrialization—creature and, perhaps, creator of our new civilization—

marched a new code of social ethics. So far as history discloses, the emergence of wives and children from the complete control of their lords and masters is very recent and nowhere else has it attained the pace America has set. Laws limiting the labor of women and children; requiring the husband and father to support his family; broadening divorce privileges and property rights; establishing compulsory education; insisting upon sanitation of homes and food; and throwing countless other protections around those whose only law had been that of the head of the house began to fill our statute books. And simultaneously, if proof were needed that this was the voluntary act of the men of the Nation, life insurance developed into a major feature of our economic structure. All this culminated almost exactly at the same time as the Eighteenth Amendment in the adoption of woman suffrage by the Nation as the free gift of men to women.

What has our economic experience been for 10 years? Well, along with all the nations of the world, we ran into a serious deflation in 1920 and 1921. Unemployment was very serious in many sections. But we got through without soup houses and recovered more rapidly than any other people, swinging into a full tide of prosperity by the end of 1922. It was this performance—and the contrasting condition among the poorer people with the condition I had observed in previous periods of unemployment—by the way, that made me a prohibitionist. From 1922 until 1929, with only very moderate declines, our production continued large and our industrial prosperity unprecedented, and this despite quite unsatisfactory conditions among our farmers and coal miners with consequent reduction of their buying power. Our efficiency in manufacture increased by leaps and bounds and the speed of our production and handling of goods. As a result we jumped the volume of our export trade enormously, proving able in many industries to undersell the world despite our vastly higher wage scale. Mass production, in its infancy in 1920, developed beyond any dreams and workmen became more and more specialists, doing their detail of the work with sureness and alertness. And thanks to the increase in productivity per man, wages mounted steadily.

Economically Beneficial

The income of the Nation increased from an estimate of $63,000,000,000 in 1921 to $89,000,000,000 for 1928. Our motor cars trebled in number; our life-insurance policyholders jumped from 13,000,000 to 27,000,000; our savings accounts from 18,000,000 in 1919 to 53,000,000 in 1929, and the amount deposited from $13,000,000,000 to $28,500,000,000.

For these statistics I must thank the fine article by Samuel Crowther in the *Ladies' Home Journal* for January [1930] entitled "Where Prohibition Is a Success." Incidentally, I am informed that Mr. Crowther started the work upon his articles, highly sceptical of the economic value of prohibition, but finished with the statement that "prohibition is an economic success."

I do not know a manufacturer—and I have talked to some who hate prohibition—who does not agree with everything I say about his workmen or who disputes the cause. I do not know a banker who does not feel prohibition to be the backbone of his savings accounts. I understand that practically every foreign economic commission which has been here to study the causes of our prosperity places prohibition first. Last summer, while abroad, two foreign manufacturers in different countries, both drinking men, told me that they were convinced that if we kept prohibition, they would have to come to it if they hoped to compete in the world's market.

A serious case is made of the nonenforcement situation— and it does look bad with graft rampant, shootings frequent, politics regnant, and the public apparently acquiescent. Well, as I have shown, none of this is new. One moving cause of great potency for the adoption of prohibition was the fact that all these things existed under the old system. The flood of illicit liquor always moved from license to no license territory. Bootleggers, like speakeasies, antedated the Volstead Act and their methods were the same.

Many Advocates of Prohibition Became Disillusioned by Its Consequences and Sought Repeal

David J. Hanson

David J. Hanson is Professor Emeritus of Sociology at the State University of New York at Potsdam. He is a well-known researcher who has served as a government consultant and has appeared on many TV programs as an expert on alcohol. In the following article he tells how people who once strongly supported Prohibition became disillusioned by the fact that it had led to increased crime, corruption, and disrespect for the law. Women, who had once thought Prohibition would make the world a safer place for their children, came to oppose it for the same reason and played a pivotal role in its repeal. In the 1932 election, in which repeal was part of the Democratic Party's platform, Prohibition was rejected by a three to one vote. However, Hanson notes, the issue remained contentious. Some state and local laws continued to prohibit the sale of alcohol, as many counties still do today.

National Prohibition in the United States had been viewed by tens of millions of Americans as the solution to the nation's poverty, crime, violence, and other ills and they eagerly embraced it. Upon establishment of the Noble Experiment in 1920, Evangelist Billy Sunday staged a mock funeral for alcoholic beverages and then extolled on the benefits of prohibition. "The reign of tears is over," he asserted. "The slums will soon be only a memory. We will turn our prisons into factories and our jails into storehouses and corncribs." Since alcohol was to be banned and since it was seen as the cause of most, if not all, crime, some communities sold their jails.

Drunk with success, temperance groups planned to extend prohibition to countries around the world. Not surprisingly, the leading prohibitionist in Congress confidently asserted that "There is as much chance of repealing the Eighteenth Amendment as there is for a hummingbird to fly to the planet Mars with the Washington Monument tied to its tail."

Unfortunately, Prohibition not only failed in its promises but actually created serious and disturbing social problems throughout society. This led to an increasing disillusionment by millions of Americans. Journalist H.L. Mencken wrote in 1925 that "Five years of prohibition have had, at le[a]st, this one benign effect: they have completely disposed of all the favorite arguments of the Prohibitionists. None of the great boons and usufructs [fruits] that were to follow the passage of the Eighteenth Amendment has come to pass. There is not less drunkenness in the Republic but more. There is not less crime, but more. There is not less insanity, but more. The cost of government is not smaller, but vastly greater. Respect for law has not increased, but diminished."

Business Leaders Disillusioned

The enthusiastic support generally given to prohibition by industrialists and business leaders had done much to prop up its support. But with the passage of time more and more business leaders became disillusioned with the consequences of the social experiment.

John D. Rockefeller, Jr., a lifelong abstainer who had contributed at least $350,000 and perhaps as much as $700,000 to the Anti-Saloon League, announced his support for repeal because of the widespread problems caused by prohibition. He explained his change of belief in a letter published in the *New York Times*:

> When the Eighteenth Amendment was passed I earnestly hoped—with a host of advocates of temperance—that it would be generally supported by public opinion and thus the day be hastened when the value to society of men with minds and bodies free from the undermining effects of alcohol would be generally realized. That this has not been the result, but rather that drinking has generally increased; that the speakeasy has replaced the saloon, not only unit for unit, but probably two-fold if not three-fold; that a vast array of lawbreakers has been recruited and financed on a colossal scale; that many of our best citizens, piqued at what they regarded as an infringement of their private rights, have openly and unabashedly disregarded the Eighteenth Amendment; that as an inevitable result respect for all law has been greatly lessened; that crime has increased to an unprecedented degree—I have slowly and reluctantly come to believe.

Henry B. Joy, past president of the Packard Motor Company, had been a very active member of the Anti-Saloon League. However, after Treasury agents repeatedly came onto his land and destroyed the property of his elderly watchman looking for illegal beer, and after they fatally shot an innocent boater who couldn't hear over his motor the demand that he stop and be searched for alcohol, Joy had seen enough. He became active in the movement to repeal prohibition. He told a Congressional committee that "I do not want my wife, my children and my grandchildren living under such conditions as exist today (under Prohibition)."

Grayson Mallet-Prevost Murphy, a private-banker and a director of Guaranty Trust Co., New York Trust Co., Bethlehem Steel, Goodyear Tire & Rubber, New York Railways, Fifth Avenue Coach Co., and the Chicago Motor Coach Co. declared: "I am opposed to Prohibition because I consider that the last ten years has shown that it is absolutely impossible to enforce. It has led to more crime, more corruption, more hypocrisy than any other law. . . . People say if you mop up the wet spots in cities the thing is done. I have never seen more vicious drinking in my life than I have seen in Indiana and in South Carolina. I have never gone anywhere in the country where the liquor law was observed. . . ." He continued that "Personally I do not know a single leading banker in the U. S., a single leading industrial executive, a single important railroad executive that I can think of who does not break this law and who does not drink."

Frederic Rene Coudert Sr., a Manhattan lawyer, stated his position strongly: "The 18th Amendment does not represent a law. . . . It is a piece of fanaticism. . . . Call out the Navy. . . . Put every citizen who violates the law into jail and have accommodations for 50 or 60 million. Then take the consequences of the government that does that of being swept out of existence."

Women Instrumental in Repeal

Women, led by the Women's Christian Temperance Union (WCTU), had been pivotal in bringing about national prohibition. Their interest had been a moral one: protecting the family, women and children from the effects of alcohol abuse. And with the passage of time it became women who proved to be pivotal in repealing prohibition. Their interest was again a moral one: prohibition was undermining the family and corrupting the morals of women and children.

In 1929, Pauline Sabin founded the Women's Legion for True Temperance, soon renamed the Women's Organization for National Prohibition Reform (WONPR). She had decided a year earlier to establish a women's repeal organization after the president of the Women's Christian Temperance Union (WCTU) asserted to Congress that "I represent the women of the United States!"

Mrs. Sabin originally supported Prohibition in the belief that "a world without liquor would be a beautiful thing" and a better place for her two sons. However, with the passage of time she became distressed at what she saw as the hypocrisy of politicians who would vote for stricter enforcement of the Eighteenth Amendment and then illegally be drinking alcohol a few minutes later, the counterproductivity of Prohibition, the decline in moderate drinking and the increase in binge drinking, the growing power of bootleggers, the widespread political corruption, mob violence, increased public intoxication, growing disrespect for law, and the erosion of personal liberty at the hands of an increasingly intrusive centralized government.

In Congressional testimony, Mrs. Sabin complained that "In preprohibition days, mothers had little fear in regard to the saloon as far as their children were concerned. A saloon-keeper's license was revoked if he was caught selling liquor to minors. Today in any speakeasy in the United States you can find boys and girls in their teens drinking liquor and this situation has become so acute that the mothers of the country feel something must be done to protect their children."

Thus, Mrs. Sabin and millions of other American women came to oppose Prohibition for the very reasons they originally supported it. They wanted the world be a safer place for their children and a better place in which to live. And women were politically infinitely more powerful than before prohibition; they were now able to vote.

As disillusionment and dissatisfaction spread, the number of repeal organizations grew. . . .

Prohibition Rejected by Voters

The demand for repeal became louder and louder. The country had entered the Great Depression, millions were unemployed, farm prices fell, tax revenues dropped, and the future looked bleak. Many believed that legalizing alcohol would increase prices for grain and other farm commodities; increase the demand for labor to produce, transport and sell alcohol; and increase taxes.

The Democratic Party platform in the 1932 election included an anti-prohibition plank and Franklin Roosevelt ran for the presidency promising repeal, which occurred on December 5, 1933. The popular vote for repeal of prohibition was 74 percent in favor and 26 percent in opposition. By a three to one vote, the American people rejected prohibition; only two states opposed repeal. A hummingbird had made the flight to Mars.

Billy Sunday had proclaimed John Barleycorn's death at the beginning of prohibition in 1920. But thirteen years later:

The cheerful spring came lightly
on,

And showers began to fall;

John Barleycorn got up again,

And sore surprised them all.

Happy throngs sang "Happy Days are Here Again!" and President [Franklin D.] Roosevelt would soon look back to what he called "The damnable affliction of Prohibition."

National prohibition had been repealed by the Twenty-first Amendment which contains two short but important sentences:

- Section 1: The eighteenth article of amendment to the Constitution of the United States is hereby repealed.

- Section 2: The transportation or importation into any State, Territory, or Possession of the United States for delivery or use therein of intoxicating liquors, in violation of the laws thereof, is hereby prohibited.

Section one made it again legal to import, produce, and sell beverage alcohol, while section two delegated to the individual states authority for regulating such beverages. Some states continued prohibition at the state level. The last state repealed it in 1966. Almost two-thirds of all states adopted some form of local option which enabled residents in political subdivisions to vote for or against local prohibition. Therefore, despite the repeal of prohibition at the national level, 38 percent of the nation's population lived in areas with state or local prohibition.

The matter of prohibition versus repeal had long been a contentious one and often divided friends and even families. It sometimes still does. Today, there are hundreds of dry (prohibition) counties across the United States seven decades after national repeal.

Impact of Amendment XVIII on Constitutional Law

Enforcing Prohibition Led to New Interpretations of Amendment IV

Robert Post

Robert Post is a professor at Yale Law School. In the following excerpt from a paper he wrote about the Supreme Court's reaction to Prohibition, he discusses two cases that have had lasting influence on American law. Post points out that it was the effort to enforce Prohibition that brought about interpretations of the Fourth Amendment that forever changed the relationship between the federal government and law enforcement. In Carroll v. United States *the Court decided that automobiles can be searched without warrants. In* Olmstead v. United States *it ruled by a narrow margin that wiretapping does not demand a warrant, either (a decision that has since been overturned), and that evidence from wiretapping can be used even when it has been illegally obtained.* Olmstead, *Post argues, created a public perception that the government was assuming new, almost unlimited powers for the sake of enforcing the Volstead Act, and Americans increasingly came to believe that the price being paid for Prohibition was too high.*

In the 1920s Americans believed themselves swept up in a crime wave of awful proportions: "Few subjects occupy more space in contemporary literature," [Harry Elmer Barnes] observed, "than analyses of the crime wave, its extent, causes and possible remedies." Solicitor General James M. Beck remarked "that the present wave of crime had no parallel since the eighteenth century." A 1926 poll named "[l]awlessness or disrespect for law" as "the greatest problem confronting this

Robert Post, "Federalism, Positivism, and the Emergence of the American Administrative State," *William and Mary Law Review*, vol. 48, October 2006, pp. 103–106, 107–109, 118–120, 122–123, 125–133, 135–143, 154, 158, 162–164, 167–168, 170–172.

country at this time." [President] Herbert Hoover made lawlessness a major theme of his new administration, announcing in his Inaugural Address that "[c]rime is increasing. Confidence in rigid and speedy justice is decreasing." Hoover pledged to meet the challenge by appointing "a national commission for a searching investigation of the whole structure of our Federal system of jurisprudence" that would "make such recommendations for reorganization of the administration of Federal laws and court procedure as may be found desirable."

Hoover was careful to stress that prohibition "was not the main source of the lawlessness" afflicting the country. Although his plea for legality was nevertheless interpreted [in a 1929 *New York Times* editorial] "as an appeal to respect the Volstead act," Hoover was correct in his perception that Americans in the 1920s were anxious about the problem of lawlessness in registers that transcend prohibition. Apart from the anxiety generated by what [Chief Justice William Howard] Taft called "[t]he great wave of crime that we have been facing," which involved not merely liquor but also an "increase of violence" like "murder and robbery," the problem of "law and order" in the 1920s was also associated with issues of labor unrest, as well as with various forms of racial violence like lynching and extralegal organizations like the Ku Klux Klan. . . .

Conflict Between Amendments

The perceived difficulty of enforcing prohibition within the constitutional restraints of the Fourth Amendment led some to advocate that the Supreme Court "recognize frankly that the 4th Amendment is inconsistent with the 18th" and "that the 4th Amendment has actually been repealed, where enforcement of the Volstead Act is concerned." At least one federal court reasoned that

> [t]he Eighteenth Amendment must be considered in determining the question of what is an unreasonable search and

Illegal Use of Alcohol Increased Rapidly During the Early Prohibition Era

Arrests for Violations of the National Prohibition Act Made by Federal Prohibition Officers

1920 (Jan. 17 to June 30)	10,548
1921	34,175
1922	42,228
1923	66,936
1924	68,161
1925	62,747

Convictions Under the National Prohibition Act in Federal Courts

1920	4,315
1921	17,962
1922	22,749
1923	34,069
1924	37,181
1925	38,498

(The above summaries do not include arrests and convictions by State authorities for prohibition offenses.)

Seizures of Illicit Distilleries, Stills, Still Worms, and Fermenters

1920 (stills only)	14,337
1921	95,933
1922	111,155
1923	158,132
1924	159,176
1925	172,537

TAKEN FROM: Statement by Senator William Cabell Bruce of Maryland, Hearings before the National Prohibition Law Subcommittee of the Committee on the Judiciary, United States Senate, April 5 to 24, 1926.

seizure as prescribed by the Fourth Amendment. If there were no Eighteenth Amendment to the Constitution to be enforced, the court might have an entirely different idea of what is an unreasonable search or seizure.... [*United States v. Bateman*]

The Taft Court, however, was not tempted by this path. Instead it sought to maintain the form of legality by affirming its commitment to both the Fourth Amendment and the exclusionary rule [the rule that evidence obtained through unconstitutional means cannot be used in court], while at the same time vigorously reinterpreting search and seizure law so as to render it compatible with the "many situations of prohibition enforcement."

The Taft Court decision that most exemplifies this approach, and that has had the most "lasting influence," is unquestionably *Carroll v. United States*. *Carroll* addressed the question of whether prohibition agents could constitutionally conduct a warrantless search of an automobile that they suspected was carrying illegal liquor. The issue of automobile searches involved "one of the most important practical difficulties in the enforcement of prohibition," because

> the passage of automobiles in pleasant weather with their tops and curtains closed and of trucks apparently loaded with furniture or other harmless freight is now so common on certain main roads in some parts of the country as to excite little comment, and the procuring of a search warrant to stop such traffic is manifestly impossible. If the officers cannot stop and search vehicles which they strongly suspect of illegal transportation they cannot stop the traffic at all and the law will be made nugatory [useless].

Carroll v. United States

The Court's opinion in *Carroll* was authored by Taft; [Justice James] McReynolds wrote a dissenting opinion joined by [Justice George] Sutherland. The case presented a new and exceedingly difficult problem that was "most important," because there was a pressing need to control criminal deployment of that "instrument of evil the automobile." In its supplemental brief the federal government had argued that "the invention, the rapid development, and the general use of automobiles" had so disturbed the "proper balance between the necessities of public authority, on the one hand, and the demands of personal liberty, on the other," that the Court had to act in order to end "the unprecedented 'crime wave.'"

The fundamental difficulty was that received constitutional doctrine did not seem adequate to cope with the challenge of the automobile. The transportation of stolen liquor in cars could not be intercepted if searches required warrants, because cars would disappear by the time any warrant could be obtained. It was generally assumed that warrantless searches were constitutional only if they were incident to a legitimate arrest. The legitimacy of an arrest was determined by reference to common law, which was understood to allow a police officer to arrest a suspect without warrant only if there was probable cause that the suspect had committed a felony, or if the suspect had, in the presence of the officer, committed a misdemeanor amounting to a breach of the peace.

The Volstead Act made transportation of illegal liquor a misdemeanor, unless the accused had been guilty of two previous violations of the Act, in which case he was guilty of a felony. Because the concealed transportation of liquor in a car was neither a "breach of the peace" committed "in the presence" of an officer, nor was it in most cases a felony, it did not seem possible to justify the search of a car as incident to a lawful arrest, even if there was probable cause to believe that the car contained unlawful liquor. Yet "the impossibility of enforcing the Eighteenth Amendment" [*United States v. Hilsinger*] was the obvious consequence of failing to find some constitutional way to allow effective searches of automobiles. Lower courts splintered badly on how to handle this problem.

Reinterpreting the Fourth

Taft constructed a solution that turned fundamentally on recognizing the authority of positive statutory law to modify traditional common law understandings. Taft began with the premise that "the main purpose" of the Volstead Act was "to reach and destroy the forbidden liquor in transportation"; "provisions for forfeiture of the vehicle and the arrest of the transporter were incidental." It did not matter whether the transporter was guilty of a misdemeanor (for his first two offenses), or of a felony (for his third offense), because the object of federal intervention was "to forfeit and suppress the liquor, the arrest of the individual being only incidental." The validity of the seizure, therefore, depended upon constitutional limits on congressional authorizations of "seizure and forfeiture" of illegal liquor. Taft rejected the theory, advanced by the defendants, that the "validity of the seizure" depended "wholly on the validity of the arrest without a seizure," holding instead that "[t]he right to search and the validity of the seizure" depended upon "[t]he rule for determining what may be required before a seizure may be made by a competent seizing official."

To determine the nature of that rule, Taft turned to a string of federal statutes beginning in the first Congress in 1789 that authorized searches of ships and other vehicles for contraband goods. Taft argued that these statutes implied

> that the guaranty of freedom from unreasonable searches and seizures by the Fourth Amendment has been construed, practically since the beginning of the Government, as recognizing a necessary difference between a search of a store, dwelling house or other structure in respect of which a proper official warrant readily may be obtained, and a search of a ship, motor boat, wagon or automobile, for contraband goods, where it is not practicable to secure a warrant because the vehicle can be quickly moved out of the locality or jurisdiction in which the warrant must be sought.

Recognizing that it "would be intolerable and unreasonable if a prohibition agent were authorized to stop every automobile on the chance of finding liquor and thus subject all persons lawfully using the highways to the inconvenience and indignity of such a search," Taft read the Volstead Act to authorize only seizures in which "the seizing officer shall have reasonable or probable cause for believing that the automobile which he stops and seizes has contraband liquor therein which is being illegally transported."

Sliding easily from the statute to the Constitution, Taft moved to the conclusion that under the Fourth Amendment

> the true rule is that if the search and seizure without a warrant are made upon probable cause, that is, upon a belief, reasonably arising out of circumstances known to the seizing officer, that an automobile or other vehicle contains that which by law is subject to seizure and destruction, the search and seizure are valid.

Taft self-consciously reached this interpretation of the Fourth Amendment "in the light of what was deemed an unreasonable search and seizure when it was adopted, and in a manner which will conserve public interests as well as the interests and rights of individual citizens." Taft's heroic effort to reinterpret Fourth Amendment doctrine in light of the pragmatic needs of law enforcement, balanced against the interests of citizens to be free from arbitrary interference, essentially set the framework for modern search and seizure jurisprudence.

Disagreement in the Court

In order to sustain his resolution of the case, Taft was forced to offer a very strained reading of the Volstead Act. Unlike the historical statutes upon which Taft based his discussion, which explicitly authorized officials to search for contraband if they had reasonable cause, the Volstead Act provided merely that

> [w]hen the commissioner, his assistants, inspectors, or any officer of the law shall discover any person in the act of transporting in violation of the law, intoxicating liquors in any wagon, buggy, automobile, water or air craft, or other vehicle, it shall be his duty to seize any and all intoxicating liquors found therein being transported contrary to law.

Taft was thus put in the awkward position of reading the term "shall discover" to mean "shall have probable cause to believe."

This was precisely the point at which McReynolds, joined by Sutherland, aimed his forceful dissent. Objecting strenuously that "[c]riminal statutes must be strictly construed and applied, in harmony with rules of the common law," McReynolds argued that "[t]he Volstead Act contains no provision which annuls the accepted common law rule or discloses definite intent to authorize arrests without warrant for misdemeanors not committed in the officer's presence." "Certainly, in a criminal statute, always to be strictly construed, the words 'shall discover . . . in the act of transporting in violation of the law,'" McReynolds contended, "cannot mean, shall have reasonable cause to suspect or believe that such transportation is being carried on. To discover and to suspect are wholly different things." The Court ought to be extraordinarily cautious, McReynolds urged, before inferring that "Congress intended to remove ancient restrictions" that circumscribed the discretion of police to arrest for misdemeanors.

In the absence of congressional authorization, the defendants' arrest was undoubtedly illegal under common law principles, and because "the seizure followed an unlawful arrest, and therefore became itself unlawful," McReynolds concluded that the evidence ought to be suppressed. "If an officer, upon mere suspicion of a misdemeanor, may stop one on the public highway, take articles away from him and thereafter use them as evidence to convict him of crime," McReynolds asked, "what becomes of the Fourth and Fifth Amendments?" . . .

Carroll seemed to imply "that a common reputation in the community of being a 'bootlegger' would justify prohibition agents in stopping and searching automobiles driven by persons thus suspected by their neighbors." It appeared to award "discretionary *carte blanche*" to prohibition officers to stop and search automobiles, and it was therefore attacked in the press [the *Washington Post*] as placing the highways:

in the power of reckless prohibition agents. A moral bad effect will be to encourage the attitude of mental lawlessness already spreading through the country like a plague. The further we go with the eighteenth amendment and the Volstead act, the deeper we get into the jungle of danger and lawlessness. . . .

Olmstead v. United States

Olmstead v. United States [is, in the words of historian David E. Kyvig] "[t]he last major Supreme Court decision concerning prohibition enforcement" and "in many ways the most controversial and significant." *Olmstead* held in 1928 that wiretapping did not constitute a search or seizure under the Fourth Amendment, and that the exclusionary rule would not apply to evidence illegally obtained, as distinct from unconstitutionally obtained. [Kyvig continues:] "Led by Chief Justice Taft . . . whose crusade for stricter enforcement of prohibition reached its zenith in this case," the Court in *Olmstead* split violently five-to-four, with Taft writing a majority opinion. . . .

Everything about *Olmstead* was dramatic and riveting. The defendant in the case, Roy Olmstead, was in 1920 the youngest and most charismatic lieutenant in the Seattle police department, who quit his day job to develop a huge and sophisticated smuggling operation that imported Canadian liquor into Washington. Known as the "king of the rumrunners," he was a popular hero in Seattle because, [according to historian Norman A. Clark],

> [h]e never corrupted his merchandise. People could trust it. He never allowed his employees to arm themselves, lecturing to them sternly that no amount of money was worth a human life. His business arrangements were conducted with a firm integrity, for he was, in his own way, a moralist. Because Olmstead was so attractive personally and because he scrupulously avoided the sordid behavior of others in the

same business—no murder, no narcotics, no rings of prostitution or gambling—many people could not regard him as an authentic criminal.

Olmstead had been convicted in federal court in 1925 largely on the basis of evidence gathered by wiretaps. At the time wiretapping was a misdemeanor under the laws of the State of Washington. In 1924 Attorney General Harlan Stone was said to have sent "a directive to the newly formed Federal Bureau of Investigation" which announced, [according to a 1952 article by William S. Fairfield and Charles Clift,] "under the heading 'Unethical Tactics,' that 'Wiretapping . . . will not be tolerated.'" But this directive would have had no effect on the Treasury Department, where prohibition enforcement was located, so that wiretapping was "the principal method used . . . to catch [prohibition] offenders." The upshot was that although wiretapping raised issues of law enforcement that were of general applicability, at the federal level the use of wiretapping was associated almost exclusively with the enforcement of prohibition.

A Divided Court

Olmstead challenged the admissibility of the wiretapping evidence. At first the Taft Court refused . . . to review his conviction, but it later reversed itself and granted [review] in a manner that limited "consideration . . . to the question whether the use of evidence of private telephone conversations, between the defendants and others, intercepted by means of wire tapping, is a violation of the Fourth and Fifth Amendments and, therefore, not permissible in the federal courts." After [the Court agreed to review the case] Assistant Attorney General Mabel Walker Willebrandt, who was in charge of prohibition enforcement at the Justice Department, withdrew from the case in protest at what she regarded as the unethical use of wiretapping.

During the two weeks before the case was argued on February 20, 1928, [Justice Louis] Brandeis, who was vehement on the question of preserving the integrity of law enforcement practices and who had been the only Justice to vote for [review] in Olmstead's original petition, prepared a memorandum that would eventually become his dissent. In its earliest versions, the memorandum began with the argument that courts ought not to admit evidence illegally procured, because courts ought not to grant redress to one who has "unclean hands." This argument, as Brandeis explicitly recognized, was distinct from the constitutional question of whether wiretapping was a search or seizure for purposes of the Fourth and Fifth Amendments. . . .

Brandeis's dissent in *Olmstead* would prove to be a profound and generative source of law because it offered . . . a theory of the "underlying purpose" of the Fourth Amendment. "The makers of our constitution," argued Brandeis, "undertook to secure conditions favorable to the pursuit of happiness. They recognized the significance of man's spiritual nature, of his feelings and of his intellect. They knew that only a part of the pain, pleasure and satisfactions of life are to be found in material things." They therefore

> sought to protect Americans in their beliefs, their thoughts, their emotions and their sensations. They conferred, as against the Government, the right to be let alone—the most comprehensive of rights and the right most valued by civilized men. To protect that right, every unjustifiable intrusion by the Government upon the privacy of the individual, whatever the means employed, must be deemed a violation of the Fourth Amendment. . . .

Brandeis did not explain why he chose to invoke the value of privacy to limit the administrative state in the context of wiretapping rather than of warrantless searches of automobiles. From a biographical perspective the explanation would no doubt lie in the violent, almost visceral disgust that Brandeis felt at the "espionage" of wiretapping. . . .

Government as Lawbreaker

Apart from the question of whether wiretapping was a search and seizure under the Fourth Amendment, *Olmstead* contained a second issue, which was not constitutional, and which had been specifically excluded by the limited grant of [review]. It was the issue, however, that from the very beginning most concerned Brandeis, and that had roused [Justice Oliver Wendell] Holmes to a dissenting opinion. It was the issue of official lawlessness, and the question was whether federal courts ought to admit evidence procured in violation of the law. Wiretapping was a misdemeanor under Washington law, and so the evidence that had convicted Olmstead was secured through what was, literally, a crime. In a short but pungent opinion, Holmes argued that the Court was not "bound" by any "body of precedents," that therefore it had "to choose, and for my part I think it a less evil that some criminals should escape than that the Government should play an ignoble part." Breaking the law by wiretapping was a "dirty business" and federal courts ought not "to allow such iniquities to succeed."

Brandeis made the same point, although more elaborately and to more brilliant rhetorical effect. He argued that by ratifying the crimes of its agents the government and its judiciary had itself become "a lawbreaker," and that federal courts should use the doctrine of clean hands to protect themselves from this danger. The court ought to exclude such evidence "in order to maintain respect for law; in order to promote confidence in the administration of justice; in order to preserve the judicial process from contamination." He concluded with an eloquent peroration that precisely evoked the widespread popular anxiety about official lawlessness and that deftly turned on Taft the Chief Justice's often stated conviction that prohibition should be enforced to maintain the rule of law:

Decency, security and liberty alike demand that government officials shall be subjected to the same rules of conduct that are commands to the citizen. In a government of laws, existence of the government will be imperilled if it fails to observe the law scrupulously. Our Government is the potent, the omnipresent teacher. For good or for ill, it teaches the whole people by its example. Crime is contagious. If the Government becomes a lawbreaker, it breeds contempt for law; it invites every man to become a law unto himself; it invites anarchy. To declare that in the administration of the criminal law the end justifies the means—to declare that the Government may commit crimes in order to secure the conviction of a private criminal—would bring terrible retribution. Against that pernicious doctrine this Court should resolutely set its face.

The upshot was that in the name of upholding the sanctity of the legal order, Taft and the Court had been maneuvered into ratifying official lawbreaking. And in the name of suppressing those who would defy the law of prohibition, they had been forced to condone a practice that was forbidden to FBI officers as "unethical" and that was at the federal level associated almost entirely with prohibition enforcement. Taft could complain that it was "bizarre" to interpret *Olmstead* as reflecting "an interest in convicting bootleggers," because "the men who voted with the majority and carried the case included men who have in a good many instances taken a view of the law which would be regarded as anti-prohibition, . . . and the other side includes Holmes and Brandeis, who have been voting to sustain the 18th Amendment vigorously in many cases." But the Court was nevertheless in an impossible position, and it made Taft bitter.

Prohibition and Government Power

It was all but inevitable that *Olmstead* would be read as an opinion carrying [as described in a *New York World* editorial] "still further the process of creating a governmental bureaucracy equipped with almost unlimited powers of espionage for the purpose of attempting to enforce Prohibition." The Court was said [by the *New York Evening Post*] to be "bewitched by Prohibition," and *Olmstead* was blasted [by *Outlook* magazine] as "the Dred Scott decision of prohibition." Most damaging, however, was the perception, hammered home by *Olmstead*, that prohibition could be imposed on a recalcitrant population only by such "detestable" practices as the "dirty business" of wiretapping. The impression left by *Olsmtead* was [according to *The Nation*] that "the heaviest load which prohibition has to carry is the shocking lawlessness that has been employed to enforce it."

In essence, the Court in *Olmstead* opted for law enforcement over the rule of law. The decision was received as confirming the view that the positive law of prohibition would be sustained by all means necessary. Attempting to explain the demise of prohibition, the historian David Kyvig has observed that "[d]uring the 1920s the Supreme Court did more than either Congress or the president to define the manner in which national prohibition would be enforced." Kyvig argues that decisions like *Olmstead* ... *[and] Carroll* ... created "[t]he image of a government prepared to engage in more aggressive and intrusive policing practices than ever before in order to enforce" prohibition. These cases confirmed the "disenchanted" perception "that government, unable to cope with lawbreakers by using traditional police methods, was assuming new powers in order to accomplish its task."

Taft's efforts to lead the Court relentlessly to sustain prohibition thus had the paradoxical effect of accentuating the disparity between the positive law of prohibition and traditional values. This disparity was most acute in the context of law enforcement, in which Americans increasingly concluded that the "experience of the last decade has shown that if we keep nationwide prohibition we shall continue to have with it summary haltings of automobiles at night, regulation of non-intoxicants, wire tapping, invasions of the home, and indiscriminate fatal shootings. These are the price we pay for prohibition." And, increasingly, Americans concluded, as did [legal scholar] Zechariah Chafee, that "the price is too high."

Searching Automobiles with Probable Cause Does Not Require a Warrant

William Howard Taft

William Howard Taft, a former law professor, was the twenty-seventh president of the United States. Some years after he left office he was appointed chief justice of the United States, which position he held from 1921 to 1930. Before the Eighteenth Amendment was adopted he opposed national prohibition, foreseeing that it would lead to a vast amount of crime and would lose the public's respect, but afterward he strongly supported its enforcement on the grounds that everyone has a duty to obey the law. In the following opinion in Carroll v. United States *he explains the Court's 5-4 ruling that it is not unconstitutional for officers to stop automobiles suspected of transporting illegal liquor and to arrest the passengers if liquor is found. Although under the Fourth Amendment, searches and seizures generally require warrants, that amendment prohibits searches and seizures only if they are unreasonable, and, he notes, it is not unreasonable in the case of moving vehicles where a warrant would be impossible to obtain. There must be probable cause, he insists, for suspecting the automobile contains liquor, but in this case there was; in his opinion the officers did not act unreasonably.*

In the passage of the supplemental Act: [to the National Prohibition Act] through the Senate, Amendment No. 32, known as the Stanley Amendment, was adopted, the relevant part of which was as follows:

> Section 6. That any officer, agent or employee of the United States engaged in the enforcement of this Act or the Na-

William Howard Taft, majority opinion, *Carroll v. United States*, U.S. Supreme Court, March 14, 1924.

tional Prohibition Act, or any other law of the United States, who shall search or attempt to search the property or premises of any person without previously securing a search warrant, as provided by law, shall be guilty of a misdemeanor and upon conviction thereof shall be fined not to exceed $1000, or imprisoned not to exceed one year, or both so fined and imprisoned in the discretion of the Court.

This Amendment was objected to in the House, and the Judiciary Committee, to whom it was referred. . . .

In its report, the Committee spoke in part as follows:

It appeared to the committee that the effect of the Senate amendment No. 32, if agreed to by the House, would greatly cripple the enforcement of the national prohibition act and would otherwise seriously interfere with the Government in the enforcement of many other laws, as its scope is not limited to the prohibition law, but applies equally to all laws where prompt action is necessary. There are on the statute books of the United States a number of laws authorizing search without a search warrant. Under the common law and agreeably to the Constitution, search may in many cases be legally made without a warrant. The Constitution does not forbid search, as some parties contend, but it does forbid unreasonable search. This provision in regard to search is, as a rule, contained in the various State constitutions, but notwithstanding that fact, search without a warrant is permitted in many cases, and especially is that true in the enforcement of liquor legislation.

The Senate amendment prohibits all search or attempt to search any property or premises without a search warrant. The effect of that would necessarily be to prohibit all search, as no search can take place if it is not on some property or premises.

Not only does this amendment prohibit search of any lands, but it prohibits the search of all property. It will prevent the search of the common bootlegger and his stock in trade, though caught and arrested in the act of violating the law. But what is perhaps more serious, it will make it impossible to stop the rum running automobiles engaged in like illegal traffic. It would take from the officers the power that they absolutely must have to be of any service, for if they cannot search for liquor without a warrant, they might as well be discharged. It is impossible to get a warrant to stop an automobile. Before a warrant could be secured, the automobile would be beyond the reach of the officer, with its load of illegal liquor disposed of.

The conference report resulted, so far as the difference between the two Houses was concerned, in providing for the punishment of any officer, agent or employee of the Government who searches a "private dwelling" without a warrant, and for the punishment of any such officer, etc., who searches any "other building or property" where, and only where, he makes the search without a warrant "maliciously and without probable cause." In other words, it left the way open for searching an automobile, or vehicle of transportation, without a warrant, if the search was not malicious or without probable cause.

The intent of Congress to make a distinction between the necessity for a search warrant in the searching of private dwellings and in that of automobiles and other road vehicles in the enforcement of the Prohibition Act is thus clearly established by the legislative history of the Stanley Amendment. Is such a distinction consistent with the Fourth Amendment? We think that it is. The Fourth Amendment does not denounce all searches or seizures, but only such as are unreasonable. . . .

Automobiles Can Be Searched

The guaranty of freedom from unreasonable searches and seizures by the Fourth Amendment has been construed, practically since the beginning of the Government, as recognizing a necessary difference between a search of a store, dwelling

Federal agents pour whiskey into a sewer. Corbis.

house or other structure in respect of which a proper official warrant readily may be obtained, and a search of a ship, motor boat, wagon or automobile, for contraband goods, where it is not practicable to secure a warrant because the vehicle can be quickly moved out of the locality or jurisdiction in which the warrant must be sought.

Having thus established that contraband goods concealed and illegally transported in an automobile or other vehicle may be searched for without a warrant, we come now to consider under what circumstances such search may be made. It would be intolerable and unreasonable if a prohibition agent were authorized to stop every automobile on the chance of finding liquor, and thus subject all persons lawfully using the highways to the inconvenience and indignity of such a search. . . . The main purpose of the Act obviously was to deal with the liquor and its transportation and to destroy it. The mere manufacture of liquor can do little to defeat the policy of the Eighteenth Amendment and the Prohibition Act, unless the forbidden product can be distributed for illegal sale and use. Section 26 was intended to reach and destroy the forbidden liquor in transportation, and the provisions for forfeiture of the vehicle and the arrest of the transporter were incidental. The rule for determining what may be required before a seizure may be made by a competent seizing official is not to be determined by the character of the penalty to which the transporter may be subjected. . . .

If an officer seizes an automobile or the liquor in it without a warrant and the facts as subsequently developed do not justify a judgment of condemnation and forfeiture, the officer may escape costs or a suit for damages by a showing that he had reasonable or probable cause for the seizure. The measure of legality of such a seizure is, therefore, that the seizing officer shall have reasonable or probable cause for believing that the automobile which he stops and seizes has contraband liquor therein which is being illegally transported.

We here find the line of distinction between legal and illegal seizures of liquor in transport in vehicles. It is certainly a reasonable distinction. It gives the owner of an automobile or other vehicle seized under Section 26, in absence of probable cause, a right to have restored to him the automobile, it protects him under the *Weeks* [*v. United States*] and *Amos* [*v. United States*] cases from use of the liquor as evidence against him, and it subjects the officer making the seizures to damages. On the other hand, in a case showing probable cause, the Government and its officials are given the opportunity, which they should have, to make the investigation necessary to trace reasonably suspected contraband goods and to seize them.

Such a rule fulfills the guaranty of the Fourth Amendment. In cases where the securing of a warrant is reasonably practicable, it must be used, and when properly supported by affidavit and issued after judicial approval, protects the seizing officer against a suit for damages. In cases where seizure is impossible except without warrant, the seizing officer acts unlawfully and at his peril unless he can show the court probable cause.

Reasonable Cause

But we are pressed with the argument that, if the search of the automobile discloses the presence of liquor and leads under the statute to the arrest of the person in charge of the automobile, the right of seizure should be limited by the common law rule as to the circumstances justifying an arrest without warrant for a misdemeanor. The usual rule is that a police officer may arrest without warrant one believed by the officer upon reasonable cause to have been guilty of a felony, and that he may only arrest without a warrant one guilty of misdemeanor if [the misdemeanor is] committed in his presence. . . .

The argument for defendants is that, as the misdemeanor to justify arrest without warrant must be committed in the presence of the police officer, the offense is not committed in his presence unless he can by his senses detect that the liquor is being transported, no matter how reliable his previous information by which he can identify the automobile as loaded with it. . . .

The language of the section provides for seizure when the officer of the law "discovers" anyone in the act of transporting the liquor by automobile or other vehicle. Certainly it is a very narrow and technical construction of this word which would limit it to what the officer sees, hears or smells as the automobile rolls by, and exclude therefrom, when he identifies the car, the convincing information that he may previously have received as to the use being made of it.

We do not think such a nice [precise] distinction is applicable in the present case. When a man is legally arrested for an offense, whatever is found upon his person or in his control which it is unlawful for him to have and which may be used to prove the offense may be seized and held as evidence in the prosecution. The argument of defendants is based on the theory that the seizure in this case can only be thus justified. If their theory were sound, their conclusion would be. The validity of the seizure then would turn wholly on the validity of the arrest without a seizure. But the theory is unsound. The right to search and the validity of the seizure are not dependent on the right to arrest. They are dependent on the reasonable cause the seizing officer has for belief that the contents of the automobile offend against the law. . . . The character of the offense for which, after the contraband liquor is found and seized, the driver can be prosecuted does not affect the validity of the seizure.

This conclusion is in keeping with the requirements of the Fourth Amendment and the principles of search and seizure of contraband forfeitable property, and it is a wise one, because it leaves the rule one which is easily applied and understood and is uniform. . . .

Finally, was there probable cause?. . .

Grand Rapids [Michigan] is about 152 miles from Detroit, and Detroit and its neighborhood along the Detroit River, which is the International Boundary, is one of the most active centers for introducing illegally into this country spirituous liquors for distribution into the interior. It is obvious from the evidence that the prohibition agents were engaged in a regular patrol along the important highways from Detroit to Grand Rapids to stop and seize liquor carried in automobiles. They knew or had convincing evidence to make them believe that the Carroll boys, as they called them, were so-called "bootleggers" in Grand Rapids, *i.e.*, that they were engaged in plying the unlawful trade of selling such liquor in that city. The officers had soon after noted their going from Grand Rapids half way to Detroit, and attempted to follow them to that city to see where they went, but they escaped observation. Two months later, these officers suddenly met the same men on their way westward, presumably from Detroit. The partners in the original combination to sell liquor in Grand Rapids were together in the same automobile they had been in the night when they tried to furnish the whisky to the officers which was thus identified as part of the firm equipment. They were coming from the direction of the great source of supply for their stock to Grand Rapids, where they plied their trade. That the officers, when they saw the defendants, believed that they were carrying liquor we can have no doubt, and we think it is equally clear that they had reasonable cause for thinking so. Emphasis is put by defendants' counsel on the statement made by one of the officers that they were not looking for defendants at the particular time when they appeared. We do not perceive that it has any weight. As soon as they did appear, the officers were entitled to use their reasoning faculties upon all the facts of which they had previous knowledge in respect to the defendants.

It is clear the officers here had justification for the search and seizure. This is to say that the facts and circumstances within their knowledge and of which they had reasonably trustworthy information were sufficient, in themselves, to warrant a man of reasonable caution in the belief that intoxicating liquor was being transported in the automobile which they stopped and searched.

Warrantless Searches of Automobiles on Mere Suspicion Are Illegal

James McReynolds

James McReynolds served on the Supreme Court from 1914 to 1941. Previously, he had been U.S. attorney general. He wrote majority opinions strongly supporting civil liberties in several important cases that have since been influential. In the following dissenting opinion in Carroll v. United States, *he argues that the Volstead Act (National Prohibition Act) did not authorize warrantless arrests and seizures and that therefore the plaintiffs' constitutional rights under the Fourth and Fifth Amendments had been violated. In this case, federal prohibition agents had attempted to buy liquor from bootleggers in order to obtain evidence against them, but no deal had been completed. Months later, the agents recognized the same bootleggers' car on the highway and stopped it, thinking that it might be transporting liquor. When they found that it was, they made an arrest. This, says McReynolds, was illegal, because they had no warrant to search and the occupants of the car were not doing anything visibly wrong at the time it was stopped—the agents suspected them merely on the basis of what had happened in the past.*

1. The damnable character of the "bootlegger's" business should not close our eyes to the mischief which will surely follow any attempt to destroy it by unwarranted methods. . . .

While quietly driving an ordinary automobile along a much frequented public road, plaintiffs in error were arrested by Federal officers without a warrant and upon mere suspicion—ill-founded, as I think. The officers then searched

James McReynolds, dissenting opinion, *Carroll v. United States*, U.S. Supreme Court, March 14, 1924.

the machine and discovered carefully secreted whisky, which was seized and thereafter used as evidence against plaintiffs in error when on trial for transporting intoxicating liquor contrary to the Volstead Act. They maintain that both arrest and seizure were unlawful, and that use of the liquor as evidence violated their constitutional rights.

This is not a proceeding to forfeit seized goods; nor is it an action against the seizing officer. . . . The Volstead Act does not, in terms, authorize arrest or seizure upon mere suspicion.

Whether the officers are shielded from prosecution or action by Rev. Stat. Sec. 970 is not important. That section does not undertake to deprive the citizen of any constitutional right, or to permit the use of evidence unlawfully obtained. It does, however, indicate the clear understanding of Congress that probable cause is not always enough to justify a seizure.

Nor are we now concerned with the question whether, by apt words, Congress might have authorized the arrest without a warrant. It has not attempted to do this. On the contrary, the whole history of the legislation indicates a fixed purpose not so to do. First and second violations are declared to be misdemeanors—nothing more—and Congress, of course, understood the rule concerning arrests for such offenses. Whether different penalties should have been prescribed or other provisions added is not for us to inquire; nor do difficulties attending enforcement give us power to supplement the legislation.

2. As the Volstead Act contains no definite grant of authority to arrest upon suspicion and without warrant for a first offense, we come to inquire whether such authority can be inferred from its provisions.

Unless the statute which creates a misdemeanor contains some clear provision to the contrary, suspicion that it is being violated will not justify an arrest. Criminal statutes must be strictly construed and applied, in harmony with rules of the common law. And the well settled doctrine is that an arrest for a misdemeanor may not be made without a warrant unless the offense is committed in the officer's presence. . . .

Warrantless Arrests Unauthorized

3. The Volstead Act contains no provision which annuls the accepted common law rule or discloses definite intent to authorize arrests without warrant for misdemeanors not committed in the officer's presence.

To support the contrary view, Section 26 is relied upon—

When . . . any officer of the law shall discover any person in the act of transporting in violation of the law, intoxicating liquors in any wagon, buggy, automobile, water or aircraft, or other vehicle, it shall be his duty to seize any and all intoxicating liquors found therein being transported contrary to law. Whenever intoxicating liquors transported or possessed illegally shall be seized by an officer, he shall take possession of the vehicle and team or automobile, boat, air or water craft, or any other conveyance, and shall arrest any person in charge thereof.

Let it be observed that this section has no special application to automobiles; it includes any vehicle—buggy, wagon, boat or air craft. Certainly, in a criminal statute, always to be strictly construed, the words "shall discover . . . in the act of transporting in violation of the law" cannot mean shall have reasonable cause to suspect or believe that such transportation is being carried on. To discover and to suspect are wholly different things. Since the beginning, apt words have been used when Congress intended that arrests for misdemeanors or seizures might be made upon suspicion. It has studiously refrained from making a felony of the offense here charged, and it did not undertake by any apt words to enlarge the power to arrest. . . .

"An Act supplemental to the National Prohibition Act," approved November 23, 1921, provides—

That any officer, agent, or employee of the United States engaged in the enforcement of this Act, or the National Prohibition Act, or any other law of the United States, who shall search any private dwelling as defined in the National Prohibition Act, and occupied as such dwelling, without a warrant directing such search, or who while so engaged shall without a search warrant maliciously and without reasonable cause search any other building or property, shall be guilty of a misdemeanor and upon conviction thereof shall be fined for a first offense not more than $1,000, and for a subsequent offense not more than $1,000 or imprisoned not more than one year, or both such fine and imprisonment.

And it is argued that the words and history of this section indicate the intent of Congress to distinguish between the necessity for warrants in order to search private dwellings and the right to search automobiles without one. Evidently Congress regarded the searching of private dwellings as matter of much graver consequence than some other searches, and distinguished between them by declaring the former criminal. But the connection between this distinction and the legality of plaintiffs in error's arrest is not apparent. Nor can I find reason for inquiring concerning the validity of the distinction under the Fourth Amendment. Of course, the distinction is valid, and so are some seizures. But what of it? The Act made nothing legal which theretofore was unlawful, and to conclude that, by declaring the unauthorized search of a private dwelling criminal, Congress intended to remove ancient restrictions from other searches and from arrests as well would seem impossible.

While the Fourth Amendment denounces only unreasonable seizures, unreasonableness often depends upon the means adopted. Here, the seizure followed an unlawful arrest, and therefore became itself unlawful—as plainly unlawful as the seizure within the home so vigorously denounced in *Weeks v. United States.*

CHICAGO COP: WHAT'VE YOU GOT IN THAT CAR?
GANGSTER: NOTHIN' BUT BOOZE, OFFICER.
COP: I BEG YOUR PARDON—I THOUGHT IT MIGHT BE HISTORY BOOKS.

A Prohibition-era cartoon shows the difficulties that police departments had enforcing the law against the manufacture, sale, and transport of alcohol in the 1920s. The Granger Collection, New York. Reproduced by permission.

In *Snyder v. United States*, the Court of Appeals, Fourth Circuit, rejected evidence obtained by an unwarranted arrest, and clearly announced some very wholesome doctrine:

That an officer may not make an arrest for a misdemeanor not committed in his presence, without a warrant, has been so frequently decided as not to require citation of authority. It is equally fundamental that a citizen may not be arrested on suspicion of having committed a misdemeanor and have his person searched by force, without a warrant of arrest. If, therefore, the arresting officer in this case had no other justification for the arrest than the mere suspicion that a bottle, only the neck of which he could see protruding from the pocket of defendant's coat, contained intoxicating liquor, then it would seem to follow without much question that the arrest and search, without first having secured a warrant, were illegal. And that his only justification was his suspicion is admitted by the evidence of the arresting officer himself. If the bottle had been empty, or if it had contained anyone of a dozen innoxious liquids, the act of the officer would, admittedly, have been an unlawful invasion of the personal liberty of the defendant. That it happened in this instance to contain whisky, we think, neither justifies the assault nor condemns the principle which makes such an act unlawful.

The validity of the seizure under consideration depends on the legality of the arrest. This did not follow the seizure, but the reverse is true. Plaintiffs in error were first brought within the officers' power, and, while therein, the seizure took place. If an officer, upon mere suspicion of a misdemeanor, may stop one on the public highway, take articles away from him, and thereafter use them as evidence to convict him of crime, what becomes of the Fourth and Fifth Amendments? . . .

Arrest Unconstitutional

The arrest of plaintiffs in error was unauthorized, illegal and violated the guarantee of due process given by the Fifth Amendment. The liquor offered in evidence was obtained by the search which followed this arrest, and was therefore obtained in violation of their constitutional rights. Articles found upon or in the control of one lawfully arrested may be used as evidence for certain purposes, but not at all when secured by the unlawful action of a Federal officer.

4. The facts known by the officers who arrested plaintiffs in error were wholly insufficient to create a reasonable belief that they were transporting liquor contrary to law. . . .

The [earlier] negotiation concerning three cases of whisky on September 29th was the only circumstance which could have subjected plaintiffs in error to any reasonable suspicion. No whisky was delivered, and it is not certain that they ever intended to deliver any. The arrest came two and a half months after the negotiation. Every act in the meantime is consistent with complete innocence. Has it come about that merely because a man once agreed to deliver whisky, but did not, he may be arrested whenever thereafter he ventures to drive an automobile on the road to Detroit!

5. When Congress has intended that seizures or arrests might be made upon suspicion, it has been careful to say so. The history and terms of the Volstead Act are not consistent with the suggestion that it was the purpose of Congress to grant the power here claimed for enforcement officers. The facts known when the arrest occurred were wholly insufficient to engender reasonable belief that plaintiffs in error were committing a misdemeanor, and the legality of the arrest cannot be supported by facts ascertained through the search which followed.

To me, it seems clear enough that the judgment should be reversed.

Evidence Obtained by Wiretapping May Be Used in Criminal Trials

William Howard Taft

William Howard Taft, a former law professor, was the twenty-seventh president of the United States. Some years after he left office he was appointed chief justice of the United States, in which position he served during most of the Prohibition era, from 1921 to 1930. In the following opinion in Olmstead v. United States, *which involved a large bootlegging operation, he explains the Court's 5-4 decision that wiretapping is not a violation of the Fourth and Fifth Amendments to the Constitution. The purpose of the Fourth Amendment ban on warrantless searches is to prevent arbitrary use of government force to enter a home and physically seize the occcupant's belongings, he argues. It cannot be extended to cover messages over external telephone wires when the home is not even entered. Furthermore, Chief Justice Taft contends, the fact that in this case wiretapping was illegal in the state where it was done has no bearing on its use in prosecuting the defendants. According to all precedent, evidence must be excluded only if constitutional rights were violated in obtaining it.* Olmstead *was the first Supreme Court case to deal with wiretapping, which was then a new technology, and the ruling was motivated by the Court's determination to enforce Prohibition. In 1967* Olmstead *was overturned by* Katz v. United States; *since then, wiretapping has required a warrant.*

The petitioners were convicted in the District Court for the Western District of Washington of a conspiracy to violate the National Prohibition Act by unlawfully possessing, transporting and importing intoxicating liquors and maintaining

William Howard Taft, majority opinion, *Olmstead v. United States*, U.S. Supreme Court, June 4, 1928.

nuisances, and by selling intoxicating liquors. Seventy-two others in addition to the petitioners were indicted. Some were not apprehended, some were acquitted, and others pleaded guilty.

The evidence in the records discloses a conspiracy of amazing magnitude to import, possess and sell liquor unlawfully. It involved the employment of not less than fifty persons, of two seagoing vessels for the transportation of liquor to British Columbia, of smaller vessels for coastwise transportation to the State of Washington, the purchase and use of a ranch beyond the suburban limits of Seattle, with a large underground cache for storage and a number of smaller caches in that city, the maintenance of a central office manned with operators, the employment of executives, salesmen, deliverymen, dispatchers, scouts, bookkeepers, collectors and an attorney. In a bad month, sales amounted to $176,000; the aggregate for a year must have exceeded two millions of dollars [about 20 million in 2007 dollars]. . . .

One of the chief men was always on duty at the main office to receive orders by telephones and to direct their filling by a corps of men stationed in another room—the "bull pen." The call numbers of the telephones were given to those known to be likely customers. At times, the sales amounted to 200 cases of liquor per day.

The information which led to the discovery of the conspiracy and its nature and extent was largely obtained by intercepting messages on the telephones of the conspirators by four federal prohibition officers. . . .

The gathering of evidence continued for many months. . . . Many of the intercepted conversations were not merely reports, but parts of the criminal acts. The evidence also disclosed the difficulties to which the conspirators were subjected, the reported news of the capture of vessels, the arrest of their men and the seizure of cases of liquor in garages and other places. It showed the dealing by Olmstead, the chief conspirator, with members of the Seattle police, the messages to them which secured the release of arrested members of the conspiracy, and also direct promises to officers of payments as soon as opportunity offered.

The Fourth Amendment provides—

> The right of the people to be secure in their persons, houses, papers, and effects against unreasonable searches and seizures shall not be violated, and no warrants shall issue but upon probable cause, supported by oath or affirmation and particularly describing the place to be searched and the persons or things to be seized.

And the Fifth: "No person . . . shall be compelled, in any criminal case, to be a witness against himself."

Only Physical Searches

It will be helpful to consider the chief cases in this Court which bear upon the construction of these Amendments. . . .

Perhaps the most important, is *Weeks v. United States,*—a conviction for using the mails to transmit coupons or tickets in a lottery enterprise. The defendant was arrested by a police officer without a warrant. After his arrest, other police officers and the United States marshal went to his house, got the key from a neighbor, entered the defendant's room and searched it, and took possession of various papers and articles. Neither the marshal nor the police officers had a search warrant. The defendant filed a petition in court asking the return of all his property. The court ordered the return of everything not pertinent to the charge, but denied return of relevant evidence. After the jury was sworn, the defendant again made objection, and, on introduction of the papers, contended that the search without warrant was a violation of the Fourth and Fifth Amendments, and they were therefore inadmissible. This court held that such taking of papers by an official of the United States, acting under color of his office, was in violation of the constitutional rights of the defendant. . . .

The striking outcome of the *Weeks* case and those which followed it was the sweeping declaration that the Fourth Amendment, although not referring to or limiting the use of evidence in courts, really forbade its introduction if obtained by government officers through a violation of the Amendment. Theretofore, many had supposed that, under the ordinary common law rules, if the tendered evidence was pertinent, the method of obtaining it was unimportant. . . . But in the *Weeks* case, and those which followed, this Court decided with great emphasis, and established as the law for the federal courts, that the protection of the Fourth Amendment would be much impaired unless it was held that not only was the official violator of the rights under the Amendment subject to action at the suit of the injured defendant, but also that the evidence thereby obtained could not be received.

The well known historical purpose of the Fourth Amendment, directed against general warrants and writs of assistance, was to prevent the use of governmental force to search a man's house, his person, his papers and his effects, and to prevent their seizure against his will. . . .

The Amendment itself shows that the search is to be of material things—the person, the house, his papers, or his effects. The description of the warrant necessary to make the proceeding lawful is that it must specify the place to be searched and the person or *things* to be seized.

It is urged that the language of Mr. Justice [Stephen Johnson] Field in *Ex parte Jackson,* already quoted, offers an analogy to the interpretation of the Fourth Amendment in respect of wiretapping. But the analogy fails. The Fourth Amendment may have proper application to a sealed letter in the mail because of the constitutional provision for the Post Office Department and the relations between the Government and those who pay to secure protection of their sealed letters. . . . It is plainly within the words of the Amendment to say that the unlawful rifling by a government agent of a sealed letter is a search and seizure of the sender's papers or effects. The letter is a paper, an effect, and in the custody of a Government that forbids carriage except under its protection.

The United States takes no such care of telegraph or telephone messages as of mailed sealed letters. The Amendment does not forbid what was done here. There was no searching. There was no seizure. The evidence was secured by the use of the sense of hearing, and that only. There was no entry of the houses or offices of the defendants.

By the invention of the telephone fifty years ago and its application for the purpose of extending communications, one can talk with another at a far distant place. The language of the Amendment cannot be extended and expanded to include telephone wires reaching to the whole world from the defendant's house or office. The intervening wires are not part of his house or office any more than are the highways along which they are stretched. . . .

Congress may, of course, protect the secrecy of telephone messages by making them, when intercepted, inadmissible in evidence in federal criminal trials by direct legislation, and thus depart from the common law of evidence. But the courts may not adopt such a policy by attributing an enlarged and unusual meaning to the Fourth Amendment. The reasonable view is that one who installs in his house a telephone instrument with connecting wires intends to project his voice to those quite outside, and that the wires beyond his house and messages while passing over them are not within the protection of the Fourth Amendment. Here, those who intercepted the projected voices were not in the house of either party to the conversation. . . .

We think, therefore, that the wiretapping here disclosed did not amount to a search or seizure within the meaning of the Fourth Amendment.

Courts May Use Illegally Obtained Evidence

What has been said disposes of the only question that comes within the terms of our order granting certiorari [review] in these cases. But some of our number, departing from that order, have concluded that there is merit in the two-fold objection overruled in both courts below—that evidence obtained through intercepting of telephone messages by government agents was inadmissible because the mode of obtaining it was unethical, and a misdemeanor under the law of Washington. To avoid any misapprehension of our views of that objection, we shall deal with it in both of its phases.

While a Territory, the English common law prevailed in Washington, and thus continued after her admission in 1889. The rules of evidence in criminal cases in courts of the United States sitting there, consequently, are those of the common law.

The common law rule is that the admissibility of evidence, is not affected by the illegality of the means by which it was obtained. . . .

The common law rule must apply in the case at bar. Nor can we, without the sanction of congressional enactment, subscribe to the suggestion that the courts have a discretion to exclude evidence the admission of which is not unconstitutional because unethically secured. This would be at variance with the common law doctrine generally supported by authority. There is no case that sustains, nor any recognized text book that gives color to, such a view. Our general experience shows that much evidence has always been receivable although not obtained by conformity to the highest ethics. The history of criminal trials shows numerous cases of prosecutions of oath-bound conspiracies for murder, robbery, and other crimes where officers of the law have disguised themselves and joined the organizations, taken the oaths and given themselves every appearance of active members engaged in the promotion of crime, for the purpose of securing evidence. Evidence secured by such means has always been received.

A standard which would forbid the reception of evidence if obtained by other than nice [precise] ethical conduct by government officials would make society suffer and give criminals greater immunity than has been known heretofore. In the absence of controlling legislation by Congress, those who realize the difficulties in bringing offenders to justice may well deem it wise that the exclusion of evidence should be confined to cases where rights under the Constitution would be violated by admitting it.

The Government Should Not Be Permitted to Break Laws Against Wiretapping

Louis Brandeis

Louis Brandeis served on the Supreme Court from 1916 to 1939, the first Jewish justice to be appointed to the Court. He was a strong advocate of privacy and his opinions have had lasting influence on the Court and on American constitutional law. The following opinion, his dissent in Olmstead v. United States, *is particularly famous and is often quoted. In it, he argues that wiretapping is a violation of the Fourth and Fifth Amendments. He also argues that the evidence in the case was obtained illegally, since wiretapping was against the law in the state in which it was obtained, and that the judgment against the defendants should therefore be reversed. The Eighteenth Amendment, he says, did not empower Congress to authorize lawbreaking, and the terms of appointment of federal Prohibition agents do not confer upon them authority to violate any criminal law. The agents were acting on their own, but when the government decided to use the illegally obtained evidence to prosecute the bootleggers, it assumed moral responsibility for their crime. In Brandeis's opinion, the Court should not allow the government to break laws in order to secure the conviction of criminals.*

The Government makes no attempt to defend the methods employed by its officers. Indeed, it concedes that, if wiretapping can be deemed a search and seizure within the Fourth Amendment, such wiretapping as was practiced in the case at bar was an unreasonable search and seizure, and that the evi-

Louis Brandeis, dissenting opinion, *Olmstead v. United States*, U.S. Supreme Court, June 4, 1928.

dence thus obtained was inadmissible. . . . But it relies on the language of the Amendment, and it claims that the protection given thereby cannot properly be held to include a telephone conversation.

"We must never forget," said Mr. Chief Justice [John] Marshall in *McCulloch v. Maryland*, "that it is a constitution we are expounding." Since then, this Court has repeatedly sustained the exercise of power by Congress, under various clauses of that instrument, over objects of which the [Founding] Fathers could not have dreamed. We have likewise held that general limitations on the powers of Government, like those embodied in the due process clauses of the Fifth and Fourteenth Amendments, do not forbid the United States or the States from meeting modern conditions by regulations which, "a century ago, or even half a century ago, probably would have been rejected as arbitrary and oppressive." *Village of Euclid v. Ambler Realty Co.* Clauses guaranteeing to the individual protection against specific abuses of power must have a similar capacity of adaptation to a changing world. . . .

When the Fourth and Fifth Amendments were adopted, "the form that evil had theretofore taken" had been necessarily simple. Force and violence were then the only means known to man by which a Government could directly effect self-incrimination. It could compel the individual to testify—a compulsion effected, if need be, by torture. It could secure possession of his papers and other articles incident to his private life—a seizure effected, if need be, by breaking and entry. Protection against such invasion of "the sanctities of a man's home and the privacies of life" was provided in the Fourth and Fifth Amendments by specific language. But "time works changes, brings into existence new conditions and purposes." *Boyd v. United States* Subtler and more far-reaching means of invading privacy have become available to the Government. Discovery and invention have made it possible for the Gov-

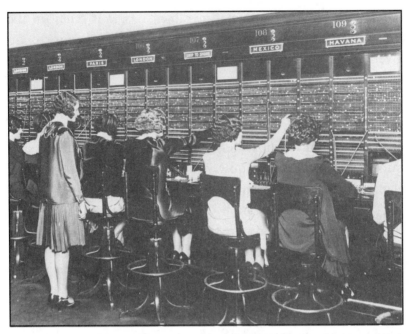

Operators at the switchboard of the American Telephone and Telegraph Company's long distance exchange. Hulton Archive/Getty Images.

ernment, by means far more effective than stretching upon the rack, to obtain disclosure in court of what is whispered in the closet.

Moreover, "in the application of a constitution, our contemplation cannot be only of what has been but of what may be." The progress of science in furnishing the Government with means of espionage is not likely to stop with wiretapping. Ways may someday be developed by which the Government, without removing papers from secret drawers, can reproduce them in court, and by which it will be enabled to expose to a jury the most intimate occurrences of the home. Advances in the psychic and related sciences may bring means of exploring unexpressed beliefs, thoughts and emotions.... Can it be that the Constitution affords no protection against such invasions of individual security?

Searches Using New Technology

A sufficient answer is found in *Boyd v. United States*, a case that will be remembered as long as civil liberty lives in the United States. This Court there reviewed the history that lay behind the Fourth and Fifth Amendments. We said with reference to Lord Camden's judgment in *Entick v. Carrington*:

> The principles laid down in this opinion affect the very essence of constitutional liberty and security. They reach farther than the concrete form of the case there before the court, with its adventitious circumstances; they apply to all invasions on the part of the Government and its employees of the sanctities of a man's home and the privacies of life. It is not the breaking of his doors, and the rummaging of his drawers, that constitutes the essence of the offence; but it is the invasion of his indefeasible right of personal security, personal liberty and private property, where that right has never been forfeited by his conviction of some public offence—it is the invasion of this sacred right which underlies and constitutes the essence of Lord Camden's judgment. Breaking into a house and opening boxes and drawers are circumstances of aggravation; but any forcible and compulsory extortion of a man's own testimony or of his private papers to be used as evidence of a crime or to forfeit his goods is within the condemnation of that judgment. In this regard, the Fourth and Fifth Amendments run almost into each other.

In *Ex parte Jackson*, it was held that a sealed letter entrusted to the mail is protected by the Amendments. The mail is a public service furnished by the Government. The telephone is a public service furnished by its authority. There is, in essence, no difference between the sealed letter and the private telephone message. As Judge [Frank H.] Rudkin said: "True, the one is visible, the other invisible; the one is tangible, the other intangible; the one is sealed, and the other unsealed, but these are distinctions without a difference."

The evil incident to invasion of the privacy of the telephone is far greater than that involved in tampering with the mails. Whenever a telephone line is tapped, the privacy of the persons at both ends of the line is invaded and all conversations between them upon any subject, and, although proper, confidential and privileged, may be overheard. Moreover, the tapping of one man's telephone line involves the tapping of the telephone of every other person whom he may call or who may call him. As a means of espionage, writs of assistance and general warrants are but puny instruments of tyranny and oppression when compared with wiretapping.

Time and again, this Court in giving effect to the principle underlying the Fourth Amendment, has refused to place an unduly literal construction upon it....

The narrow language of the Amendment has been consistently construed in the light of its object, "to insure that a person should not be compelled, when acting as a witness in any investigation, to give testimony which might tend to show that he himself had committed a crime. The privilege is limited to criminal matters, but it is as broad as the mischief against which it seeks to guard." *Counselman v. Hitchcock* ...

The protection guaranteed by the Amendments is much broader in scope. The makers of our Constitution undertook to secure conditions favorable to the pursuit of happiness. They recognized the significance of man's spiritual nature, of his feelings, and of his intellect. They knew that only a part of the pain, pleasure and satisfactions of life are to be found in material things. They sought to protect Americans in their beliefs, their thoughts, their emotions and their sensations. They conferred, as against the Government, the right to be let alone—the most comprehensive of rights, and the right most valued by civilized men. To protect that right, every unjustifiable intrusion by the Government upon the privacy of the individual, whatever the means employed, must be deemed a violation of the Fourth Amendment. And the use, as evidence in a criminal proceeding, of facts ascertained by such intrusion must be deemed a violation of the Fifth.

Applying to the Fourth and Fifth Amendments the established rule of construction, the defendants' objections to the evidence obtained by wiretapping must, in my opinion, be sustained. It is, of course, immaterial where the physical connection with the telephone wires leading into the defendants' premises was made. And it is also immaterial that the intrusion was in aid of law enforcement. Experience should teach us to be most on our guard to protect liberty when the Government's purposes are beneficent. Men born to freedom are naturally alert to repel invasion of their liberty by evil-minded rulers. The greatest dangers to liberty lurk in insidious encroachment by men of zeal, well meaning but without understanding.

Government Lawbreaking Not to Be Condoned

Independently of the constitutional question, I am of opinion that the judgment should be reversed. By the laws of Washington, wiretapping is a crime. To prove its case, the Government was obliged to lay bare the crimes committed by its officers on its behalf. A federal court should not permit such a prosecution to continue. . . .

The evidence obtained by crime was obtained at the Government's expense, by its officers, while acting on its behalf; the officers who committed these crimes are the same officers who were charged with the enforcement of the Prohibition Act; the crimes of these officers were committed for the purpose of securing evidence with which to obtain an indictment and to secure a conviction. The evidence so obtained constitutes the warp and woof of the Government's case. . . . There is literally no other evidence of guilt on the part of some of the defendants except that illegally obtained by these officers. As to nearly all the defendants (except those who admitted guilt), the evidence relied upon to secure a conviction consisted mainly of that which these officers had so obtained by violating the state law.

As Judge Rudkin said: "Here we are concerned with neither eavesdroppers nor thieves. Nor are we concerned with the acts of private individuals. . . . We are concerned only with the acts of federal agents whose powers are limited and controlled by the Constitution of the United States."

The Eighteenth Amendment has not, in terms, empowered Congress to authorize anyone to violate the criminal laws of a State. And Congress has never purported to do so. The terms of appointment of federal prohibition agents do not purport to confer upon them authority to violate any criminal law. . . .

When these unlawful acts were committed, they were crimes only of the officers individually. The Government was innocent, in legal contemplation, for no federal official is authorized to commit a crime on its behalf. When the Government, having full knowledge, sought, through the Department of Justice, to avail itself of the fruits of these acts in order to accomplish its own ends, it assumed moral responsibility for the officers' crimes. And if this Court should permit the Government, by means of its officers' crimes, to effect its purpose of punishing the defendants, there would seem to be present all the elements of a ratification. If so, the Government itself would become a lawbreaker.

Will this Court, by sustaining the judgment below, sanction such conduct on the part of the Executive? The governing principle has long been settled. It is that a court will not redress a wrong when he who invokes its aid has unclean hands. . . .

Decency, security and liberty alike demand that government officials shall be subjected to the same rules of conduct that are commands to the citizen. In a government of laws, existence of the government will be imperiled if it fails to observe the law scrupulously. Our Government is the potent, the omnipresent teacher. For good or for ill, it teaches the whole people by its example. Crime is contagious. If the Government becomes a lawbreaker, it breeds contempt for law; it invites every man to become a law unto himself; it invites anarchy. To declare that, in the administration of the criminal law, the end justifies the means—to declare that the Government may commit crimes in order to secure the conviction of a private criminal—would bring terrible retribution. Against that pernicious doctrine this Court should resolutely set its face.

CONSTITUTIONAL
AMENDMENTS
BEYOND THE BILL OF RIGHTS

CHAPTER 3

Impact of Amendment XXI on Constitutional Law

Amendment XXI Interacts with Other Provisions of the Constitution

Johnny H. Killian et al.

The following article is a portion of a document prepared by the Congressional Research Service of the Library of Congress. This section analyzes cases decided by the U.S. Supreme Court in terms of how the Twenty-first Amendment to the Constitution was interpreted. Most of these decisions involved the importation of liquor from one state to another, which the Twenty-first Amendment gave the individual states full power to control. However, there have also been cases that deal with how the Twenty-first Amendment affects other provisions of the Constitution. Generally the Court ruled that it does not override the Bill of Rights nor the Fourteenth Amendment, although state bans on sexually explicit entertainment and topless dancing in establishments seeking liquor licenses were upheld in two cases. The Twenty-first Amendment does not affect antitrust laws that forbid price fixing. And it does not bar the federal government from making grants of highway funds conditional on a state raising the minimum drinking age.

In a series of interpretive decisions rendered shortly after ratification of the Twenty-first Amendment, the Court established the proposition that States are competent to adopt legislation discriminating against imported intoxicating liquors in favor of those of domestic origin and that such discrimination offends neither the commerce clause of Article I nor the equal protection and due process clauses of the Fourteenth Amendment. Thus, in *State Board of Equalization v.*

The Constitution of the United States, Analysis and Interpretation. Washington, DC: U.S. Government Printing Office, 2004. www.gpoaccess.gov/constitution/pdf2002/039.pdf.

Young's Market Co., a California statute was upheld which exacted a $500 annual license fee for the privilege of importing beer from other States and a $750 fee for the privilege of manufacturing beer; and in *Mahoney v. Triner Corp.*, a Minnesota statute was sustained which prohibited a licensed manufacturer or wholesaler from importing any brand of intoxicating liquor containing more than 25 percent alcohol by volume and ready for sale without further processing, unless such brand was registered in the United States Patent Office. . . .

Conceding, in *State Board of Equalization v. Young's Market Co.*, that "prior to the Twenty-first Amendment it would obviously have been unconstitutional to have imposed any fee for . . . the privilege of importation . . . even if the State had exacted an equal fee for the privilege of transporting domestic beer from its place of manufacture to the [seller's] place of business," the Court proclaimed that this Amendment "abrogated the right to import free, so far as concerns intoxicating liquors." Inasmuch as the Amendment was viewed as conferring on states an unconditioned authority to prohibit totally the importation of intoxicating beverages, it logically followed that any discriminatory restriction falling short of total exclusion was equally valid, notwithstanding the absence of any connection between such restriction and public health, safety or morals. As to the contention that the unequal treatment of imported beer would contravene the equal protection clause, the Court succinctly observed that a "classification recognized by the Twenty-first Amendment cannot be deemed forbidden by the Fourteenth."

In *Seagram & Sons v. Hostetter* the Court upheld a state statute regulating the price of intoxicating liquors, asserting that the Twenty-first Amendment bestowed upon the States broad regulatory power over the liquor sales within their territories. . . . The Court added that there was nothing in the Twenty-first Amendment or any other part of the Constitu-

Per Capita Consumption of Alcoholic Beverages (Gallons of Pure Alcohol) 1910–1929

Consumption of alcohol surpassed the level of the years immediately preceding the Eighteenth Amendment long before that amendment was repealed. It had been declining throughout the decade before Prohibition went into effect, but though it fell significantly during the first two years of Prohibition, it soon rebounded.

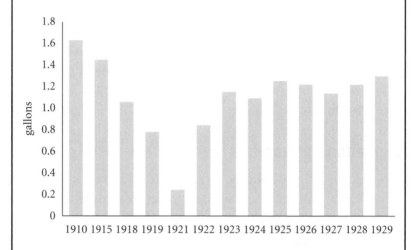

TAKEN FROM: Clark Warburton, *The Economic Results of Prohibition.* New York: Columbia University Press, 1932.

tion that required state laws regulating the liquor business to be motivated exclusively by a desire to promote temperance.

Recent cases have undercut the expansive interpretation of state powers in the *Young's Market* and *Triner Corp.* cases. Twenty-first Amendment and [the Constitution's] commerce clause principles are to be harmonized where possible. The Court now phrases the question in terms of "whether the interests implicated by a state regulation are so closely related to the powers reserved by the Twenty-first Amendment that the regulation may prevail, notwithstanding that its requirements directly conflict with express federal policies." . . .

Regulation of Interstate Liquor Traffic

When passing upon the constitutionality of legislation regulating the carriage of liquor interstate, a majority of the Justices seemed disposed to by-pass the Twenty-first Amendment and to resolve the issue exclusively in terms of the commerce clause and state power. . . .

A total eclipse of the Twenty-first Amendment was recorded in *Duckworth v. Arkansas* and *Carter v. Virginia*, wherein, without even considering that Amendment, a majority of the Court upheld, as not contravening the commerce clause, statutes regulating the transport through the State of liquor cargoes originating and ending outside the regulating State's boundaries.

Regulation of Imports

Importation of alcoholic beverages into a State for ultimate delivery at a National Park located therein but over which the United States retained exclusive jurisdiction has been construed as not constituting "transportation . . . into [a] State for delivery and use therein" within the meaning of § 2 of the Amendment. The importation having had as its objective delivery and use in a federal area over which the State retained no jurisdiction, the increased powers which the State acquired from the Twenty-first Amendment were declared to be inapplicable. California therefore could not extend the importation license and other regulatory requirements of its Alcoholic Beverage Control Act to a retail liquor dealer doing business in the Park. . . .

Imports and Exports

The Twenty-first Amendment did not repeal the export-import clause, nor obliterate the commerce clause. Accordingly, a State cannot tax imported Scotch whiskey while it remains "in unbroken packages in the hands of the original importer and prior to [his] resale or use" thereof. Likewise, New York is precluded from terminating the business of an airport dealer who, under sanction of federal customs laws, acquired "tax-free liquors for export" from out-of-state sources for resale exclusively to airline passengers, with delivery deferred until the later arrive at foreign destinations. Similarly, a state "affirmation law" prohibiting wholesalers from charging lower prices on out-of-state sales than those already approved for in-state sales is invalid as a direct regulation of interstate commerce. "The Commerce Clause operates with full force whenever one State attempts to regulate the transportation and sale of alcoholic beverages destined for distribution and consumption in a foreign country . . . or another State."

Effect of Section 2

Nothwithstanding the 1936 assertion that "[a] classification recognized by the Twenty-first Amendment cannot be deemed forbidden by the Fourteenth," the Court has now in a series of cases acknowledged that § 2 of the Twenty-first Amendment did not repeal provisions of the Constitution adopted before ratification of the Twenty-first, save for the severe cabining of commerce clause application to the liquor traffic, but it has formulated no consistent rationale for a determination of the effect of the later provision upon earlier ones. In *Craig v. Boren*, the Court invalidated a state law that prescribed different minimum drinking ages for men and women as violating the equal protection clause. To the State's Twenty-first Amendment argument, the Court replied that the Amendment "primarily created an exception to the normal operation of the Commerce Clause" and that its "relevance . . . to other constitutional provisions" is doubtful. "'Neither the text nor the history of the Twenty-first Amendment suggests that it qualifies individual rights protected by the Bill of Rights and the Fourteenth Amendment where the sale or use of liquor is concerned.'" The square holding on this point is "that the operation of the Twenty-first Amendment does not alter the application of the equal protection standards that would otherwise govern this case." Other decisions reach the same result but without discussing the application of the Amendment. Similarly, a state "may not exercise its power under the Twenty-first Amendment in a way which impinges upon the Establishment Clause of the First Amendment."

The Court departed from this line of reasoning in *California v. LaRue*. There, the Court sustained the facial constitutionality of regulations barring a lengthy list of actual or simulated sexual activities and motion picture portrayals of these activities in establishments licensed to sell liquor by the drink. In an action attacking the validity of the regulations as applied to ban nude dancing in bars, the Court considered at some length the material adduced at the public hearings which resulted in the rules demonstrating the anti-social consequences of the activities in the bars. It conceded that the regulations reached expression that would not be deemed legally obscene under prevailing standards and reached expressive conduct that would not be prohibitable under prevailing standards, but the Court thought that the constitutional protection of conduct that partakes "more of gross sexuality than of communication" was outweighed by the State's interest in maintaining order and decency. Moreover, the Court continued, the second section of the Twenty-first Amendment gave an "added presumption in favor of the validity" of the regulations as applied to prohibit questioned activities in places serving liquor by the drink.

A much broader ruling was forthcoming when the Court considered the constitutionality of a state regulation banning topless dancing in bars. "Pursuant to its power to regulate the sale of liquor within its boundaries, it has banned topless dancing in establishments granted a license to serve liquor. The State's power to ban the sale of alcoholic beverages entirely includes the lesser power to ban the sale of liquor on premises where topless dancing occurs." This recurrence to the greater-includes-the-lesser-power argument, relatively rare in recent years, would, if it were broadly applied, give the States in the area of regulation of alcoholic beverages a review-free discretion of unknown scope.

In *44 Liquormart, Inc. v. Rhode Island*, the Court disavowed *LaRue* . . . and reaffirmed that, "although the Twenty-first Amendment limits the effect of the dormant Commerce Clause on a state's regulatory power over the delivery or use of intoxicating beverages within its borders, 'the Amendment does not license the States to ignore their obligations under other provisions of the Constitution,'" and therefore does not afford a basis for state legislation infringing freedom of expression protected by the First Amendment. There is no reason, the Court asserted, for distinguishing between freedom of expression and the other constitutional guarantees (e.g., those protected by the Establishment and Equal Protection Clauses) held to be insulated from state impairment pursuant to powers conferred by the Twenty-first Amendment. The Court hastened to add by way of dictum that states retain adequate police powers to regulate "grossly sexual exhibitions in premises licensed to serve alcoholic beverages." "Entirely apart from the Twenty-first Amendment, the State has ample power to prohibit the sale of alcoholic beverages in inappropriate locations."

Effect on Federal Regulation

The Twenty-first Amendment does not oust all federal regulatory power affecting transportation or sale of alcoholic beverages. Thus, the Court held, the Amendment does not bar a prosecution under the Sherman Antitrust Act of producers, wholesalers, and retailers charged with conspiring to fix and maintain retail prices of alcoholic beverages in Colorado. . . .

Following a review of the cases in this area, the Court has observed "that there is no bright line between federal and state powers over liquor. The Twenty-first Amendment grants the States virtually complete control over whether to permit importation or sale of liquor and how to structure the liquor distribution system. Although States retain substantial discretion to establish other liquor regulations, those controls may be subject to the federal commerce power in appropriate situations. The competing state and federal interests can be reconciled only after careful scrutiny of those concerns in a 'concrete case.'" Invalidating under the Sherman Act a state fair trade scheme imposing a resale price maintenance policy for wine, the Court balanced the federal interest in free enterprise expressed through the antitrust laws against the asserted state interests in promoting temperance and orderly marketing conditions. Since the state courts had found the policy under attack promoted neither interest significantly, the Supreme Court experienced no difficulty in concluding that the federal interest prevailed.

Congress may condition receipt of federal highway funds on a state's agreeing to raise the minimum drinking age to 21, the Twenty-first Amendment not constituting an "independent constitutional bar" to this sort of spending power exercise even though Congress may lack the power to achieve its purpose directly.

States May Ban Sexually Explicit Entertainment in Establishments with Liquor Licenses

William H. Rehnquist

William H. Rehnquist became a justice of the U.S. Supreme Court in 1972, and in 1986 he became chief justice, a position he held until his death in 2005. He was a strong conservative who believed in a strict interpretation of the Constitution. In the following majority opinion in the case of California v. LaRue, *he states that the Twenty-first Amendment gives states the power to regulate conduct in establishments to which liquor licenses are granted. California's Department of Alcoholic Beverage Control had denied licenses to nightclubs offering sexually explicit entertainment. The nightclubs, along with some of the dancers who performed there, filed suit on the grounds that this was a violation of their constitutional right of free speech, and they were upheld by a lower court. The Supreme Court, however, decided that because their conduct had not been forbidden by law but merely made grounds for refusal of a liquor license, the regulations were not unreasonable and did not violate the Constitution.*

Appellees include holders of various liquor licenses issued by [the California Department of Alcoholic Beverage Control], and dancers at premises operated by such licensees. In 1970, the Department promulgated rules regulating the type of entertainment that might be presented in bars and nightclubs that it licensed. . . .

Concerned with the progression in a few years' time from "topless" dancers to "bottomless" dancers and other forms of

William H. Rehnquist, majority opinion, *California v. LaRue*, U.S. Supreme Court, December 5, 1972.

"live entertainment" in bars and nightclubs that it licensed, the Department heard a number of witnesses on this subject at public hearings held prior to the promulgation of the rules. . . .

References to the transcript of the hearings submitted by the Department to the District Court indicated that in licensed establishments where "topless" and "bottomless" dancers, nude entertainers, and films displaying sexual acts were shown, numerous incidents of legitimate concern to the Department had occurred. . . .

Prostitution occurred in and around such licensed premises, and involved some of the female dancers. Indecent exposure to young girls, attempted rape, rape itself, and assaults on police officers took place on or immediately adjacent to such premises. . . .

Shortly before the effective date of the Department's regulations, appellees unsuccessfully sought discretionary review of them in both the State Court of Appeal and the Supreme Court of California. The Department then joined with appellees in requesting the three-judge District Court to decide the merits of appellees' claims that the regulations were invalid under the Federal Constitution.

The District Court majority upheld the appellees' claim that the regulations in question unconstitutionally abridged the freedom of expression guaranteed to them by the First and Fourteenth Amendments to the United States Constitution. It reasoned that the state regulations had to be justified either as a prohibition of obscenity in accordance with the *Roth* [*v. United States*] line of decisions in this Court, or else as a regulation of "conduct" having a communicative element in it under the standards laid down by this Court in *United States v. O'Brien*. Concluding that the regulations would bar some entertainment that could not be called obscene under the *Roth* line of cases, and that the governmental interest being furthered by the regulations did not meet the tests laid down in *O'Brien*, the court enjoined the enforcement of the regulations.

An Issue of Liquor Licensing, Not Censorship

The state regulations here challenged come to us not in the context of censoring a dramatic performance in a theater, but rather in a context of licensing bars and nightclubs to sell liquor by the drink. In *Seagram & Sons v. Hostetter*, this Court said:

> Consideration of any state law regulating intoxicating beverages must begin with the Twenty-first Amendment, the second section of which provides that:

> The transportation or importation into any State, Territory, or possession of the United States for delivery or use therein of intoxicating liquors, in violation of the laws thereof, is hereby prohibited.

While the States, vested as they are with general police power, require no specific grant of authority in the Federal Constitution to legislate with respect to matters traditionally within the scope of the police power, the broad sweep of the Twenty-first Amendment has been recognized as conferring something more than the normal state authority over public health, welfare, and morals. In *Hostetter v. Idlewild Liquor Corp.*, the Court reaffirmed that, by reason of the Twenty-first Amendment, "a State is totally unconfined by traditional Commerce Clause limitations when it restricts the importation of intoxicants destined for use, distribution, or consumption within its borders."

Still earlier, the Court stated in *State Board v. Young's Market Co.*, "A classification recognized by the Twenty-first Amendment cannot be deemed forbidden by the Fourteenth."

These decisions did not go so far as to hold or say that the Twenty-first Amendment supersedes all other provisions of the United States Constitution in the area of liquor regulations. In *Wisconsin v. Constantineau*, the fundamental notice and hearing requirement of the Due Process Clause of the Fourteenth Amendment was held applicable to Wisconsin's statute providing for the public posting of names of persons who had engaged in excessive drinking. But the case for upholding state regulation in the area covered by the Twenty-first Amendment is undoubtedly strengthened by that enactment: "Both the Twenty-first Amendment and the Commerce Clause are parts of the same Constitution. Like other provisions of the Constitution, each must be considered in the light of the other and in the context of the issues and interests at stake in any concrete case." *Hostetter v. Idlewild Liquor Corp.*

A common element in the regulations struck down by the District Court appears to be the Department's conclusion that the sale of liquor by the drink and lewd or naked dancing and entertainment should not take place in bars and cocktail lounges for which it has licensing responsibility. Based on the evidence from the hearings that it cited to the District Court, and mindful of the principle that, in legislative rulemaking, the agency may reason from the particular to the general, we do not think it can be said that the Department's conclusion in this respect was an irrational one.

Appellees insist that the same results could have been accomplished by requiring that patrons already well on the way to intoxication be excluded from the licensed premises. But wide latitude as to choice of means to accomplish a permissible end must be accorded to the state agency that is itself the repository of the State's power under the Twenty-first Amendment. Nothing in the record before us or in common experience compels the conclusion that either self-discipline on the part of the customer or self-regulation on the part of the bartender could have been relied upon by the Department to secure compliance with such an alternative plan of regulation. The Department's choice of a prophylactic solution instead of one that would have required its own personnel to judge individual instances of inebriation cannot, therefore, be deemed an unreasonable one under the holdings of our prior cases.

The State's Authority

We do not disagree with the District Court's determination that these regulations on their face would proscribe some forms of visual presentation that would not be found obscene under *Roth* and subsequent decisions of this Court. But we do not believe that the state regulatory authority in this case was limited to either dealing with the problem it confronted within the limits of our decisions as to obscenity, or in accordance with the limits prescribed for dealing with some forms of communicative conduct in *O'Brien*.

Our prior cases have held that both motion pictures and theatrical productions are within the protection of the First and Fourteenth Amendments. . . .

But as mode of expression moves from the printed page to the commission of the public acts that may themselves violate valid penal statutes, the scope of permissible state regulations significantly increases. States may sometimes proscribe expression that is directed to the accomplishment of an end that the State has declared to be illegal when such expression consists, in part, of "conduct" or "action." In *O'Brien*, the Court suggested that the extent to which "conduct" was protected by the First Amendment depended on the presence of a "communicative element," and stated: "We cannot accept the view that an apparently limitless variety of conduct can be labeled 'speech' whenever the person engaging in the conduct intends thereby to express an idea."

The substance of the regulations struck down prohibits licensed bars or nightclubs from displaying, either in the form of movies or live entertainment, "performances" that partake more of gross sexuality than of communication. While we agree that at least some of the performances to which these regulations address themselves are within the limits of the constitutional protection of freedom of expression, the critical fact is that California has not forbidden these performances across the board. It has merely proscribed such performances in establishments that it licenses to sell liquor by the drink.

Viewed in this light, we conceive the State's authority in this area to be somewhat broader than did the District Court. This is not to say that all such conduct and performance are without the protection of the First and Fourteenth Amendments. But we would poorly serve both the interests for which the State may validly seek vindication and the interests protected by the First and Fourteenth Amendments were we to insist that the sort of bacchanalian revelries that the Department sought to prevent by these liquor regulations were the constitutional equivalent of a performance by a scantily clad ballet troupe in a theater.

The Department's conclusion, embodied in these regulations, that certain sexual performances and the dispensation of liquor by the drink ought not to occur at premises that have licenses was not an irrational one. Given the added presumption in favor of the validity of the state regulation in this area that the Twenty-first Amendment requires, we cannot hold that the regulations on their face violate the Federal Constitution.

Amendment XXI Does Not Override the Right to Freedom of Speech

Thurgood Marshall

Thurgood Marshall was the first African American to serve as a justice of the Supreme Court. He was a strong supporter of individual rights. In the following dissenting opinion in California v. LaRue, *he argues that the regulations regarding sexually explicit entertainment used by California's Department of Alcoholic Beverage Control to deny liquor licenses are too broad, and would make no distinction between pornography and artistic masterpieces. He says that although states have power to regulate the distribution of liquor, that power may not be exercised in a way that abridges freedom of speech. In his opinion, the Twenty-first Amendment deals only with the authority of the states to prevent the importation of liquor—it was intended merely to permit "dry" states to control the flow of liquor across their boundaries. There is no indication that Congress meant it to tamper with First Amendment rights. Furthermore, the regulations discriminate on the basis of the content of speech, as nightclubs are allowed to present live shows and movies on all topics except sex without losing their liquor licenses. For these reasons, he believes that the regulations are unconstitutional even though they apply only to eligibility for a liquor license and do not involve criminal penalties if they are not followed.*

In my opinion, the District Court's judgment should be affirmed. The record in this case is not a pretty one, and it is possible that the State could constitutionally punish some of the activities described therein under a narrowly drawn scheme. . . . I think it clear that the regulations are overbroad,

Thurgood Marshall, dissenting opinion, *California v. LaRue*, U.S. Supreme Court, December 5, 1972.

and therefore unconstitutional. Although the State's broad power to regulate the distribution of liquor and to enforce health and safety regulations is not to be doubted, that power may not be exercised in a manner that broadly stifles First Amendment freedoms. . . .

It should be clear at the outset that California's regulatory scheme does not conform to the standards which we have previously enunciated for the control of obscenity. . . . In *Roth* [*v. the United States*], we held . . . "judging obscenity by the effect of isolated passages upon the most susceptible persons, might well encompass material legitimately treating with sex, and so it must be rejected as unconstitutionally restrictive of the freedoms of speech and press."

Instead, we held that the material must be "taken as a whole," and, when so viewed, must appeal to a prurient interest in sex, patently offend community standards relating to the depiction of sexual matters, and be utterly without redeeming social value.

Obviously, the California rules do not conform to these standards. They do not require the material to be judged as a whole, and do not speak to the necessity of proving prurient interest, offensiveness to community standards, or lack of redeeming social value. Instead of the contextual test approved in *Roth* and *Memoirs* [*v. Massachusetts*], these regulations create a system of *per se* rules to be applied regardless of context: certain acts simply may not be depicted and certain parts of the body may under no circumstances be revealed. The regulations thus treat on the same level a serious movie such as "Ulysses" and a crudely made "stag film." They ban not only obviously pornographic photographs, but also great sculpture from antiquity.

Roth held 15 years ago [in 1957] that the suppression of serious communication was too high a price to pay in order to vindicate the State's interest in controlling obscenity, and I see no reason to modify that judgment today. Indeed, even the appellants do not seriously contend that these regulations can be justified under the *Roth-Memoirs* test. Instead, appellants argue that California's regulations do not concern the control of pornography at all. These rules, they argue, deal with conduct, rather than with speech, and, as such, are not subject to the strict limitations of the First Amendment. . . .

Performances Constitutionally Protected

If, as . . . many cases hold, movies, plays, and the dance enjoy constitutional protection, it follows, ineluctably, I think, that their component parts are protected as well. It is senseless to say that a play is "speech" within the meaning of the First Amendment, but that the individual gestures of the actors are "conduct" which the State may prohibit. The State may no more allow movies while punishing the "acts" of which they are composed than it may allow newspapers while punishing the "conduct" of setting type.

Of course, I do not mean to suggest that anything which occurs upon a stage is automatically immune from state regulation. No one seriously contends, for example, that an actual murder may be legally committed so long as it is called for in the script, or that an actor may inject real heroin into his veins while evading the drug laws that apply to everyone else. But once it is recognized that movies and plays enjoy *prima facie* First Amendment protection, the standard for reviewing state regulation of their component parts shifts dramatically. . . .

In order to restrict speech, the State must show that the speech is "used in such circumstances and [is] of such a nature as to create a clear and present danger that [it] will bring about the substantive evils that [the State] has a right to prevent." (*Schenck v. United States*)

When the California regulations are measured against this stringent standard, they prove woefully inadequate. Appellants defend the rules as necessary to prevent sex crimes, drug abuse, prostitution, and a wide variety of other evils. These are precisely the same interests that have been asserted time and again before this Court as justification for laws banning frank discussion of sex, and that we have consistently rejected. In fact, the empirical link between sex-related entertainment and the criminal activity popularly associated with it has never been proved and, indeed, has now been largely discredited. Yet even if one were to concede that such a link existed, it would hardly justify a broad-scale attack on First Amendment freedoms. . . .

Limits of Twenty-first Amendment

But California contends that these regulations do not involve suppression at all. The State claims that its rules are not regulations of obscenity, but are rather merely regulations of the sale and consumption of liquor. Appellants point out that California does not punish establishments which provide the proscribed entertainment, but only requires that they not serve alcoholic beverages on their premises. Appellants vigorously argue that such regulation falls within the State's general police power as augmented, when alcoholic beverages are involved, by the Twenty-first Amendment.

I must confess that I find this argument difficult to grasp. To some extent, it seems premised on the notion that the Twenty-first Amendment authorizes the States to regulate liquor in a fashion which would otherwise be constitutionally impermissible. But the Amendment, by its terms, speaks only to state control of the importation of alcohol, and its legislative history makes clear that it was intended only to permit "dry" States to control the flow of liquor across their boundaries despite potential Commerce Clause objections. There is not a word in that history which indicates that Congress meant to tamper in any way with First Amendment rights. I submit that the framers of the Amendment would be astonished to discover that they had inadvertently enacted a *pro tanto* [only to a certain extent] repealer of the rest of the Constitution. Only last Term, we held that the State's conceded power to license the distribution of intoxicating beverages did not justify use of that power in a manner that conflicted with the Equal Protection Clause. I am at a loss to understand why the Twenty-first Amendment should be thought to override the First Amendment, but not the Fourteenth.

To be sure, state regulation of liquor is important, and it is deeply embedded in our history. But First Amendment values are important as well. Indeed, in the past, they have been thought so important as to provide an independent restraint on every power of Government. "Freedom of press, freedom of speech, freedom of religion are in a preferred position." *(Murdock v. Pennsylvania)* Thus, when the Government attempted to justify a limitation on freedom of association by reference to the war power, we categorically rejected the attempt. "[The] concept of 'national defense,'" we held, "cannot be deemed an end in itself, justifying any exercise of legislative power designed to promote such a goal."...

If the First Amendment limits the means by which our Government can ensure its very survival, then surely it must limit the State's power to control the sale of alcoholic beverages as well.

Of course, this analysis is relevant only to the extent that California has, in fact, encroached upon First Amendment rights. Appellants argue that no such encroachment has occurred, since appellees are free to continue providing any entertainment they choose without fear of criminal penalty. Appellants suggest that this case is somehow different because all that is at stake is the "privilege" of serving liquor by the drink.

Absense of Criminal Sanctions

It should be clear, however, that the absence of criminal sanctions is insufficient to immunize state regulation from constitutional attack. On the contrary, "this is only the beginning, not the end, of our inquiry." *(Sherbert v. Verner)* For "[i]t is too late in the day to doubt that the liberties of religion and expression may be infringed by the denial of or placing of conditions upon a benefit or privilege." . . .

Thus, unconstitutional conditions on welfare benefits, unemployment compensation, tax exemptions, public employment, bar admissions, and mailing privileges have all been invalidated by this Court. In none of these cases were criminal penalties involved. In all of them, citizens were left free to exercise their constitutional rights so long as they were willing to give up a "gratuity" that the State had no obligation to provide. Yet, in all of them, we found that the discriminatory provision of a privilege placed too great a burden on constitutional freedoms. I therefore have some difficulty in understanding why California nightclub proprietors should be singled out and informed that they alone must sacrifice their constitutional rights before gaining the "privilege" to serve liquor.

Of course, it is true that the State may, in proper circumstances, enact a broad regulatory scheme that incidentally restricts First Amendment rights. For example, if California prohibited the sale of alcohol altogether, I do not mean to suggest that the proprietors of theaters and bookstores would be constitutionally entitled to a special dispensation. But, in that event, the classification would not be speech-related, and hence could not be rationally perceived as penalizing speech. Classifications that discriminate against the exercise of constitutional rights *per se* stand on an altogether different footing. They must be supported by a "compelling" governmental purpose, and must be carefully examined to insure that the purpose is unrelated to mere hostility to the right being asserted.

Moreover, not only is this classification speech related; it also discriminates between otherwise indistinguishable parties on the basis of the content of their speech. Thus, California nightclub owners may present live shows and movies dealing with a wide variety of topics while maintaining their licenses. But if they choose to deal with sex, they are treated quite differently. Classifications based on the content of speech have long been disfavored, and must be viewed with the gravest suspicion. . . .

We have said that "[t]he door barring federal and state intrusion into this area cannot be left ajar; it must be kept tightly closed, and opened only the slightest crack necessary to prevent encroachment upon more important interests" *Roth v. United States*. Because I can see no reason why we should depart from that standard in this case, I must respectfully dissent.

Amendment XXI Is Irrelevant to the Raising of the Drinking Age

William H. Rehnquist

William H. Rehnquist became a justice of the U.S. Supreme Court in 1972 and in 1986, chief justice, a position he held until his death in 2005. He was a strong conservative who believed in a strict interpretation of the Constitution. In the following majority opinion in South Dakota v. Dole, *he states that although there is controversy about whether the Twenty-first Amendment would permit enactment of a national drinking age, the Court does not have to decide that issue because this case involves merely the federal government's spending power. Congress does have the right to attach conditions to states' receipt of federal funds, he says, provided that these conditions meet certain criteria. They must, among other things, be related to the program being funded. The Court decided that making highway funds conditional on a state's raising of the drinking age to twenty-one is related to highways because when the drinking age is inconsistent between states, young people drive across state borders in order to drink legally. The Twenty-first Amendment does not prevent the federal government from setting conditions involving the sale of alcohol, Rehnquist argues, since the power to enact laws regarding its sale remains with the states, and they will lose only a small percentage of highway funding if they decide not to comply.*

Petitioner South Dakota permits persons 19 years of age or older to purchase beer containing up to 3.2% alcohol. In 1984, Congress enacted 23 U.S.C. § 158 which directs the Secretary of Transportation to withhold a percentage of federal highway funds otherwise allocable from States "in which the

William H. Rehnquist, majority opinion, *South Dakota v. Dole*, U.S. Supreme Court, June 23, 1987.

purchase or public possession . . . of any alcoholic beverage by a person who is less than twenty-one years of age is lawful." The State sued in United States District Court seeking a declaratory judgment that § 158 violates the constitutional limitations on congressional exercise of the spending power and violates the Twenty-first Amendment to the United States Constitution. The District Court rejected the State's claims, and the Court of Appeals for the Eighth Circuit affirmed.

In this Court, the parties direct most of their efforts to defining the proper scope of the Twenty-first Amendment, relying on our statement in *California Retail Liquor Dealers Assn. v. Midcal Aluminum,* that the "Twenty-first Amendment grants the States virtually complete control over whether to permit importation or sale of liquor and how to structure the liquor distribution system."

South Dakota asserts that the setting of minimum drinking ages is clearly within the "core powers" reserved to the States under § 2 of the Amendment. Section 158, petitioner claims, usurps that core power. The Secretary, in response, asserts that the Twenty-first Amendment is simply not implicated by § 158; the plain language of § 2 confirms the States' broad power to impose restrictions on the sale and distribution of alcoholic beverages, but does not confer on them any power to permit sales that Congress seeks to *prohibit.* That Amendment, under this reasoning, would not prevent Congress from affirmatively enacting a national minimum drinking age more restrictive than that provided by the various state laws; and it would follow *a fortiori* [with even more convincing force] that the indirect inducement involved here is compatible with the Twenty-first Amendment.

These arguments present questions of the meaning of the Twenty-first Amendment, the bounds of which have escaped precise definition. Despite the extended treatment of the question by the parties, however, we need not decide in this case whether that Amendment would prohibit an attempt by Con-

Justice William Rehnquist served on the U.S. Supreme Court as chief justice from 1986 until his death in 2005. © Wally McNamee/Corbis.

gress to legislate directly a national minimum drinking age. Here, Congress has acted indirectly under its spending power to encourage uniformity in the States' drinking ages. As we explain below, we find this legislative effort within constitutional bounds even if Congress may not regulate drinking ages directly.

Conditions on Receipt of Federal Funds

The Constitution empowers Congress to "lay and collect Taxes, Duties, Imposts, and Excises, to pay the Debts and provide for the common Defence and general Welfare of the United States."

Incident to this power, Congress may attach conditions on the receipt of federal funds, and has repeatedly employed the power "to further broad policy objectives by conditioning receipt of federal moneys upon compliance by the recipient with federal statutory and administrative directives." *(Fullilove v. Klutznick)* . . .

Thus, objectives not thought to be within Article I's "enumerated legislative fields," may nevertheless be attained through the use of the spending power and the conditional grant of federal funds.

The spending power is of course not unlimited, but is instead subject to several general restrictions articulated in our cases. The first of these limitations is derived from the language of the Constitution itself: the exercise of the spending power must be in pursuit of "the general welfare." In considering whether a particular expenditure is intended to serve general public purposes, courts should defer substantially to the judgment of Congress. Second, we have required that, if Congress desires to condition the States' receipt of federal funds, it "must do so unambiguously . . . enabl[ing] the States to exercise their choice knowingly, cognizant of the consequences of their participation." *(Pennhurst State School and Hospital v. Halderman)* Third, our cases have suggested (without significant elaboration) that conditions on federal grants might be illegitimate if they are unrelated "to the federal interest in particular national projects or programs." *(Massachusetts v. United States)*

South Dakota does not seriously claim that § 158 is inconsistent with any of the first three restrictions mentioned above. We can readily conclude that the provision is designed to serve the general welfare, especially in light of the fact that "the concept of welfare or the opposite is shaped by Congress. . . ." *(Helvering v. Davis)* Congress found that the differing drinking ages in the States created particular incentives for young persons to combine their desire to drink with their ability to drive, and that this interstate problem required a national solution. The means it chose to address this dangerous situation were reasonably calculated to advance the general welfare. The conditions upon which States receive the funds, moreover, could not be more clearly stated by Congress. And the State itself, rather than challenging the germaneness of the condition to federal purposes, admits that it "has never contended that the congressional action was . . . unrelated to a national concern in the absence of the Twenty-first Amendment." Indeed, the condition imposed by Congress is directly related to one of the main purposes for which highway funds are expended—safe interstate travel. This goal of the interstate highway system had been frustrated by varying drinking ages among the States. A Presidential commission appointed to study alcohol-related accidents and fatalities on the Nation's highways concluded that the lack of uniformity in the States' drinking ages created "an incentive to drink and drive" because "young persons commut[e] to border States where the drinking age is lower." By enacting § 158, Congress conditioned the receipt of federal funds in a way reasonably calculated to address this particular impediment to a purpose for which the funds are expended.

The remaining question about the validity of § 158—and the basic point of disagreement between the parties—is whether the Twenty-first Amendment constitutes an "independent constitutional bar" to the conditional grant of federal funds. Petitioner, relying on its view that the Twenty-first Amendment prohibits *direct* regulation of drinking ages by Congress, asserts that "Congress may not use the spending power to regulate that which it is prohibited from regulating directly under the Twenty-first Amendment."

But our cases show that this "independent constitutional bar" limitation on the spending power is not of the kind petitioner suggests. *United States v. Butler*, for example, established that the constitutional limitations on Congress when exercising its spending power are less exacting than those on its authority to regulate directly. . . .

No Great Loss

We think that the language in our earlier opinions stands for the unexceptionable proposition that the power may not be used to induce the States to engage in activities that would themselves be unconstitutional. Thus, for example, a grant of federal funds conditioned on invidiously discriminatory state action or the infliction of cruel and unusual punishment would be an illegitimate exercise of the Congress' broad spending power. But no such claim can be or is made here. Were South Dakota to succumb to the blandishments offered by Congress and raise its drinking age to 21, the State's action in so doing would not violate the constitutional rights of anyone.

Our decisions have recognized that, in some circumstances, the financial inducement offered by Congress might be so coercive as to pass the point at which "pressure turns into compulsion." *(Steward Machine Co. v. Davis)* Here, however, Congress has directed only that a State desiring to establish a minimum drinking age lower than 21 lose a relatively small percentage of certain federal highway funds. Petitioner contends that the coercive nature of this program is evident from the degree of success it has achieved. We cannot conclude, however, that a conditional grant of federal money of this sort is unconstitutional simply by reason of its success in achieving the congressional objective.

When we consider, for a moment, that all South Dakota would lose if she adheres to her chosen course as to a suitable minimum drinking age is 5% of the funds otherwise obtainable under specified highway grant programs, the argument as to coercion is shown to be more rhetoric than fact. . . .

Here Congress has offered relatively mild encouragement to the States to enact higher minimum drinking ages than they would otherwise choose. But the enactment of such laws remains the prerogative of the States not merely in theory, but in fact. Even if Congress might lack the power to impose a national minimum drinking age directly, we conclude that encouragement to state action found in § 158 is a valid use of the spending power.

The Federal Government Cannot Raise the Drinking Age Even by Withholding Funds

Sandra Day O'Connor

Sandra Day O'Connor was the first woman justice of the Supreme Court, where she served from 1981 until her retirement in 2006. As a swing vote between its conservative and liberal factions, she was often extremely influential. In the following dissenting opinion in South Dakota v. Dole, *she maintains that Congress is not entitled to make receipt of federal highway funds conditional on states raising the drinking age to twenty-one. The argument that this enhances highway safety is not valid, she contends, because in the first place it prevents teenagers from drinking even when they are not about to drive, and in the second place because teens account for only a small proportion of drunken drivers. Therefore, she concludes, the condition is not sufficiently related to highway use to justify interfering with the power to regulate the sale of liquor given to the states by the Twenty-first Amendment.*

The Court today upholds the National Minimum Drinking Age Amendment, 23 U.S.C. § 158 . . . as a valid exercise of the spending power conferred by Article I, § 8 [of the Constitution]. But § 158 is not a condition on spending reasonably related to the expenditure of federal funds, and cannot be justified on that ground. Rather, it is an attempt to regulate the sale of liquor, an attempt that lies outside Congress' power to regulate commerce because it falls within the ambit of § 2 of the Twenty-first Amendment.

My disagreement with the Court is relatively narrow on the spending power issue: it is a disagreement about the appli-

Sandra Day O'Connor, dissenting opinion, *South Dakota v. Dole*, U.S. Supreme Court, June 23, 1987.

cation of a principle, rather than a disagreement on the principle itself. I agree with the Court that Congress may attach conditions on the receipt of federal funds to further "the federal interest in particular national projects or programs." *(Massachusetts v. United States)* I also subscribe to the established proposition that the reach of the spending power "is not limited by the direct grants of legislative power found in the Constitution." *(United States v. Butler)* Finally, I agree that there are four separate types of limitations on the spending power: the expenditure must be for the general welfare, the conditions imposed must be unambiguous, they must be reasonably related to the purpose of the expenditure, and the legislation may not violate any independent constitutional prohibition. Insofar as two of those limitations are concerned, the Court is clearly correct that § 158 is wholly unobjectionable. Establishment of a national minimum drinking age certainly fits within the broad concept of the general welfare, and the statute is entirely unambiguous. I am also willing to assume, *arguendo* [for the sake of argument] that the Twenty-first Amendment does not constitute an "independent constitutional bar" to a spending condition.

But the Court's application of the requirement that the condition imposed be reasonably related to the purpose for which the funds are expended is cursory and unconvincing. We have repeatedly said that Congress may condition grants under the spending power only in ways reasonably related to the purpose of the federal program. In my view, establishment of a minimum drinking age of 21 is not sufficiently related to interstate highway construction to justify so conditioning funds appropriated for that purpose.

In support of its contrary conclusion, the Court relies on a supposed concession by counsel for South Dakota that the State "has never contended that the congressional action was ... unrelated to a national concern in the absence of the Twenty-first Amendment." In the absence of the Twenty-first

Amendment, however, there is a strong argument that the Congress might regulate the conditions under which liquor is sold under the commerce power, just as it regulates the sale of many other commodities that are in or affect interstate commerce. The fact that the Twenty-first Amendment is crucial to the State's argument does not, therefore, amount to a concession that the condition imposed by § 158 is reasonably related to highway construction. . . .

Aside from these "concessions" by counsel, the Court asserts the reasonableness of the relationship between the supposed purpose of the expenditure—"safe interstate travel"—and the drinking age condition. The Court reasons that Congress wishes that the roads it builds may be used safely, that drunken drivers threaten highway safety, and that young people are more likely to drive while under the influence of alcohol under existing law than would be the case if there were a uniform national drinking age of 21. It hardly needs saying, however, that, if the purpose of § 158 is to deter drunken driving, it is far too over- and under-inclusive. It is overinclusive because it stops teenagers from drinking even when they are not about to drive on interstate highways. It is underinclusive because teenagers pose only a small part of the drunken driving problem in this Nation.

Outside the Ken of Congress

When Congress appropriates money to build a highway, it is entitled to insist that the highway be a safe one. But it is not entitled to insist as a condition of the use of highway funds that the State impose or change regulations in other areas of the State's social and economic life because of an attenuated or tangential relationship to highway use or safety. Indeed, if the rule were otherwise, the Congress could effectively regulate almost any area of a State's social, political, or economic life on the theory that use of the interstate transportation system is somehow enhanced. If, for example, the United States were to condition highway moneys upon moving the state capital, I suppose it might argue that interstate transportation is facilitated by locating local governments in places easily accessible to interstate highways—or, conversely, that highways might become overburdened if they had to carry traffic to and from the state capital. In my mind, such a relationship is hardly more attenuated than the one which the Court finds supports § 158. . . .

As discussed above, a condition that a State will raise its drinking age to 21 cannot fairly be said to be reasonably related to the expenditure of funds for highway construction. The only possible connection, highway safety, has nothing to do with how the funds Congress has appropriated are expended. Rather than a condition determining how federal highway money shall be expended, it is a regulation determining who shall be able to drink liquor. As such, it is not justified by the spending power.

Of the other possible sources of congressional authority for regulating the sale of liquor, only the commerce power comes to mind. But in my view, the regulation of the age of the purchasers of liquor, just as the regulation of the price at which liquor may be sold, falls squarely within the scope of those powers reserved to States by the Twenty-first Amendment. As I emphasized in *324 Liquor Corp. v. Duffy*: "The history of the Amendment strongly supports Justice [Hugo] Black's view that the Twenty-first Amendment was intended to return absolute control of the liquor trade to the States, and that the Federal Government could not use its Commerce Clause powers to interfere in any manner with the States' exercise of the power conferred by the Amendment." Accordingly, Congress simply lacks power under the Commerce Clause to displace state regulation of this kind.

The immense size and power of the Government of the United States ought not obscure its fundamental character. It remains a Government of enumerated powers. Because 23

U.S.C. § 158 cannot be justified as an exercise of any power delegated to the Congress, it is not authorized by the Constitution. The Court errs in holding it to be the law of the land, and I respectfully dissent.

CONSTITUTIONAL
AMENDMENTS
BEYOND THE BILL OF RIGHTS

CHAPTER 4

Current Relevance of Amendments XVIII and XXI

Prohibition Failed Once and It Is Failing Again

Peter Christ

*Peter Christ is a retired police captain and a founder of Law En-
forcement Against Prohibition (LEAP). In the following article
he argues that prohibition of drugs is failing for the same reasons that prohibition of alcohol did, and that it should be ended.
In his opinion, prohibition gives control of drugs to criminal organizations and it leads to corruption in law enforcement. Punishment will never stop drug abuse, he contends; the billions that
the government wastes each year in the war on drugs should be
diverted to education. Many police officers, prosecutors, judges,
and others are now joining LEAP because their experience has
led them to agree.*

The Shinnecock Indian Nation recently was the target of a
multi-agency raid in which drugs, weapons and cash resulted in the arrest of 13 people on the eastern Long Island
reservation and in other local communities. Since [President]
Richard Nixon's declaration of a war on drugs more than
three decades ago, our nation is still awash in drugs, which are
more abundant and cheaper now than they were then. We
have tried to arrest our way out of our drug abuse problems
and we have only netted more abuse, more violence and more
corruption—in other words, we have failed.

I am a retired police officer, with a 20-year career that saw
me reach the rank of captain. In my years of policing, there
was a common theme that kept appearing. In spite of all our
arrests, in spite of our detailed investigations and locking up
plenty of drug dealers, we never really won. Each arrest only

created a job opening which was soon filled. This is a story constantly played out across our nation.

The drug war—or to be more clear, Prohibition II—is a failure of policy that has wreaked havoc upon our communities, whether it be the Shinnecock Nation or any American town or city. This prohibition exhibits all the failures of our earlier 20th century prohibition of alcohol. We have corruption running rampant in law enforcement, from the smallest community police forces to the former commander of our military forces in Colombia.

Criminals Control Drugs

Rather than stymie the production or distribution of illegal drugs, prohibition actually places control of illegal drugs directly into the hands of criminal organizations. Criminals have no codes or regulations that stop them from selling to children or from marketing drugs cut with often toxic impurities.

It must be understood that in denouncing prohibition and calling for its end, we do not advocate for drug use—just the opposite. Drug abuse is not something punishment will ever end. People are human beings with all the failures, all the moles and warts that come with being human. So we must find another way. And it is my belief and a belief held by many other criminal justice professionals that we need to legalize and thus regulate and control all drugs.

Being a police officer carries a great responsibility. We are entrusted with the duty of ensuring community safety and of being examples to our communities. Prohibition however, damages the implied integrity of wearing the badge because the cash, the power, the drugs themselves too often prove too large a temptation to ignore. Good cops are in the overwhelming majority of our police forces but there are enough that fall prey to the lure of easy bucks to tarnish every officer's badge.

So do we continue down the same path? Should we continue locking up more of our young people, watching more families devastated by the problems of rampant drugs and the subsequent drug abuse? Or should we change directions? Should we do what was done when the failures of alcohol prohibition finally forced us into ending that disaster?

I believe we must change direction. We must find a different path. That is why we are so enthused about Law Enforcement Against Prohibition. LEAP is an organization only five years old [as of 2007] but now consisting of more than 8,000 members, many of whom are former criminal justice professionals, representing the spectrum of law enforcement. Judges, cops, prosecutors, Customs and Border Protection, corrections and others are joining us because their professional experience, often as frontline warriors in the drug war, has led them to the same conclusions.

Only by ending prohibition will we ever remove criminals from the equation. By ending the drug war we can redistribute the $70 billion or so the federal government wastes each year in its failed war on drugs. We know that programs utilizing truthful education are more effective than policies using half-truths and hubris as their cornerstones. For example, education has been very effective in reducing tobacco consumption.

Drug abuse is bad. But the war on drugs fails to curb abuse. It is time for a change. Prohibition failed once and we ended it. It has failed again and it is time to end it again.

The Failure of Prohibition Should Not Guide Today's Drug Policy

U.S. Department of Justice

The following article is an excerpt from a Drug Enforcement Administration (an office of the U.S. Department of Justice) manual offering rebuttals to common arguments in favor of legalizing drugs. It contends that the arguments of drug legalization advocates who compare the war on drugs to Prohibition are not valid because there are great differences between the Prohibition era and the situation today. There was no public consensus about prohibiting alcohol, whereas now the vast majority of citizens believe drugs should remain illegal, the manual argues. During Prohibition, only the sale of alcohol was illegal, while today drug users can be targeted. Criminal penalties are more severe today than in the Prohibition era. Drugs are prohibited internationally, whereas alcohol was not. Furthermore, Prohibition was not as great a failure as it is generally believed to have been—in many ways it was successful and, the department maintains, it did not cause an increase in the crime rate.

Proponents of legalization suggest that the United States experience with alcohol prohibition in the 1920's provides ample proof of the problems that result when the government attempts to make a popular substance illegal. Legalizers point to ostensible increases in organized crime such as that associated with Al Capone in order to make their point. Basically, they say, it is better to legalize, tax and regulate than simply to declare drugs illegal.

The legalizers' arguments here are deeply flawed and merit two primary responses: first, the circumstances surrounding

Tom Pool, *Drug Legalization, Myths and Misconceptions*. Washington, DC: U.S. Department of Justice. www.druglibrary.org/schaffer/debate/myths/myths6.htm.

Prohibition are so different than those of today's world that it practically is impossible to use its history as a means of analyzing present-day policy; second, Prohibition was in fact successful and did not create the negative consequences that the legalizers say it did.

But to the first point. David Teasley, an analyst with the Congressional Research Service of the Library of Congress, undertook an in-depth analysis in 1992 entitled, "Drug legalization and the 'lessons' of Prohibition." Teasley ultimately concluded that

> [A] comprehensive analogy between Prohibition and the modern drug problem is problematic in at least two major ways. First, between the two eras there are significant differences that tend to undermine the prolegalization analogy. Second, many arguments of the prolegalizers are weakened by their reliance upon a widely held set of popular beliefs about Prohibition rather than upon recent historical evidence. Such attempts to create this analogy based upon these popular beliefs about Prohibition serve only to confuse the debate over legalization of illicit drugs.

Let us examine the differences that Teasley (and others) cite between the era of Prohibition and the era in which we now live.

Conditions Unlike Today's

First, during prohibition the government sought to restrict the consumption of alcohol although it lacked the moral consensus of the nation. That is, even during Prohibition, most people were accepting of alcohol. Such is not the case today, for the vast majority of citizens do feel that illicit drugs should remain illegal. Thus, Prohibition went against the national consensus whereas illegalization of drugs does not.

Second, the laws of Prohibition themselves were different than those dealing with illicit drugs today. During Prohibition, it was not illegal to drink alcohol, it was only illegal to sell it. Today, however, it is both illegal to sell and to use illicit drugs. Consequently, today's laws can target the users while those of the Prohibition era could not.

Third, during the Prohibition era several states did not support the federal laws. This fact created tension between the state and federal governments and hampered effective prosecution of alcohol distributors. Today, 48 states have signed the Uniform Controlled Substances Act, and all are in effective agreement with the federal government in matters of drug policy—a state/federal consensus exists that was not present during Prohibition.

Fourth, criminal penalties are much more severe today than in the 1920's. For example, the first-offense bootlegger faced a maximum fine of $1,000 or six months in prison. Today, a first-offense trafficker of cocaine or heroin (of less than 100 grams) faces fines up to $1 million and imprisonment for up to 20 years.

Fifth, during Prohibition the United States was a "dry" nation within a "wet" international community. Just as the Prohibition policies were counter to the moral consensus within the U.S., they were also at odds with that of the international community (which explains why so much alcohol was imported from Canada). But . . . the international community is resolute when it comes to drug policy; in December of 1988 over 80 countries signed the Convention Against Illicit Traffic in Narcotic Drugs and Psychotropic Substances.

Sixth and finally, the administrative structure of the government agencies designed to carry out the Prohibition laws was narrow, unstable, and filled with political appointees. Today's national drug strategy involves over a dozen federal agencies coordinated by the Office of National Drug Control Policy. In short, the governmental bodies that prosecute today's drug violators are much larger, have much better resources, and are much more professional than their Prohibition counterparts.

Barry McCaffrey, the fourth director of the Office of National Drug Control Policy, holds a booklet titled "Plan Colombia" while speaking to reporters in Washington D.C. The booklet outlined plans to end drug trafficking and guerrilla warfare in Colombia. © Reuters NewMedia Inc./Corbis. Reproduced by permission.

Prohibition Met Its Goals

Thus, it is factually incorrect for the legalizers to analogize our history with Prohibition to today's drug policies. They simply do not have that much in common. But should the legalizers choose to make such an analogy, they also should be made aware of the fact that Prohibition was on balance a successful program.

First, use of alcohol decreased significantly during Prohibition. This decrease in turn led to a marked decrease in the incidence of cirrhosis of the liver. Also, alcohol-related arrests decreased 50%. Finally, the suicide rate also decreased by 50%.

A second reason why Prohibition was a successful program is due to the fact that it did not—contrary to popular myth—cause an increase in the crime rate. It is true that there was an increase in the homicide rate during Prohibition, but this is not the same as an increase in the overall crime rate. Furthermore, the increase in homicide occurred predominantly in the African-American community, and African-Americans at that time were not the people responsible for alcohol trafficking. The drama of [prohibition agent] Elliot Ness and [gangster] Al Capone largely was just that, drama sensationalized by the media of the time.

In short, it is doubtful that one legitimately may analogize Prohibition with our current efforts to control drugs. There are too many differences in the laws, the political establishment, the moral consensus, and the international community to make such analogizing worthwhile. Nonetheless, the fact remains that Prohibition accomplished many of its goals, improved the health of the entire nation, and did not cause a significant increase in the crime rate. Mark Kleiman, who has proposed legalizing marijuana, notes, the U.S. experience with Prohibition is the best evidence to support the continued illegalization of illicit drugs.

The War on Drugs Is Creating the Same Problems Prohibition Did

Johann Hari

Johann Hari is an award-winning journalist who writes for the Independent, *one of Britain's leading newspapers, and many other major papers worldwide. In the following article, published shortly after the death of Nobel Prize–winning economist Milton Friedman, he describes Friedman's opposition to the prohibition of drugs. Friedman grew up during the Prohibition era and saw how it failed to reduce alcohol abuse yet led to the rise of criminal gangs. He foresaw how the war on drugs would create even more crime and would cause people to use more dangerous forms of drugs than they would in a legal market. He also warned that globalizing the war on drugs would globalize gangsterism and result in the destruction of other countries. However, Hari says, this does not mean that Friedman was in favor of drug use. He believed that heavy drug use is a great evil, but that the measures being used against it are a major source of such use. In Hari's opinion, the failure of drug prohibition will soon become undeniable, and it may then be ended quickly, just as alcohol prohibition was.*

Over forty years, [Nobel Prize–winning economist Milton Friedman] offered the most devastating slap-downs of the "war on drugs" ever written.

Friedman was a child when alcohol was criminalised in America. The Prohibitionist crusade to banish the "demon rum" and dry out the United States lasted until he was in his twenties. The lessons lasted his lifetime. He saw that even when you use force—the police and army—to try to physically prevent people from using a popular intoxicant, you don't actually reduce its use very much. "I wasn't very old and was not much of a drinker but there was no difficulty in finding speakeasies," he explained. The most generous estimate is that alcohol consumption fell by a fifth initially, and then rose to pre-prohibition levels as people discovered surreptitious channels for a mouthful of moonshine.

But while prohibition didn't succeed in the fantasies of its fans that it would "end alcoholism", it did succeed gloriously in one respect. It handed a massive, popular industry to armed criminal gangs, who succeeded to ramp up the murder rate by 78 percent and make a mockery of the rule of law. "We had this spectacle of Al Capone, of the hijackings, of the gang wars ..." Friedman wrote. "Prohibition is an attempted cure that makes matters worse—for both the addict and the rest of us."

Prohibition Creates Gangsters

Friedman saw—way ahead of almost any other commentator—how prohibiting cannabis, cocaine and heroin would spawn a thousand Capones. He warned, "Al Capone epitomises our earlier attempt at Prohibition; the Crips and Bloods epitomise this one." The old Chicago gangster famously gunned down six of his alcohol-hawking competitors on the St Valentine's Day Massacre in 1929. But in the age of drug prohibition, there are equivalent dealer shoot-outs every minute of the day in South Central Los Angeles—and Hackney [England], and Bogata [Colombia], and Kabul [Afghanistan]. People without recourse to the law will protect their property with hard ammunition. Late in his life, Friedman calculated that 10,000 people were dying every year in the US alone as a direct result of these killings, equivalent to more than three September 11ths. Most were bystanders caught in the cross-fire.

Milton Friedman, a Nobel Prize–winning economist, grew up during the Prohibition era. Friedman believed Prohibition did not reduce alcohol abuse; rather, he found it increased criminal gang activity. Archive Photos, Inc./Camera Press, Ltd. Reproduced by permission.

And by globalising this Puritan war on drugs, the US government has globalised this gangsterism. Friedman warned that the war on drugs has "undermined the very foundations of Colombian society" and "condemned hundreds, perhaps thousands, of Colombians to violent death." I have just returned from Mexico, which is rapidly Colombianising, with whole areas controlled by dealers who bribe or out-gun the police force and terrorise the local population. The same thing is happening on a huge scale in Afghanistan. "By what right do we destroy other people's countries just because we cannot enforce our own laws?" Friedman asked.

But armed gangsters are not the only species of crime generated by prohibition. In his careful, methodical style, Friedman proved that criminalising drugs causes an explosion in muggings and burglary, making us all victims of this war at some time in our lives. How? A kilo of heroin passes through six different dealers in the supply chain before it reaches the veins of a Londoner. Each link in the chain demands a fat fee for risking jail. This means heroin costs 3000 percent more than it would in a legal, risk-free market—and a heroin addict must steal 3000 percent more to buy it. 3000 percent more grannies mugged, 3000 percent more homes burgled.

That's why so many police officers are now coming out in favour of unpicking hardline prohibition and prescribing heroin to addicts. . . . They know from the experience in Switzerland—an ultra-conservative country that now nonetheless prescribes heroin—that it is a silver bullet (or syringe?), bringing crime rates crashing down.

This does not mean Friedman was in favour of drugs. One of the biggest problems with the legalisation brand is that it is still contaminated by the legacy of idiots like [psychologist and LSD guru] Timothy O'Leary, who thought drug use was an active good, an act of liberation. (Go visit a heroin addict in rehab and tell them how liberated they are). By contrast, Friedman thought (rightly) that heavy drug use—whether it was alcoholism, cannabis-addiction or junkiedom—was a human disaster. He once told Bill Bennett, [President George

H.W.] Bush's drug tsar, "You are not mistaken in believing that drugs are a scourge that is devastating our society. Your mistake is failing to recognise that the very measures you favour are a major source of the evils you deplore."

More Dangerous Drugs

Friedman proved, for example, that prohibition changes the way people use drugs, making many people use stronger, more dangerous variants than they would in a legal market. During alcohol prohibition, moonshine eclipsed beer; during drug prohibition, crack is eclipsing coke. He called his rule explaining this curious historical fact "the Iron Law of Prohibition": the harder the police crack down on a substance, the more concentrated the substance will become.

Why? If you run a bootleg bar in Prohibition-era Chicago and you are going to make a gallon of alcoholic drink, you could make a gallon of beer, which one person can drink and constitutes one sale—or you can make a gallon of pucheen, which is so strong it takes thirty people to drink it and constitutes thirty sales. Prohibition encourages you to produce and provide the stronger, more harmful drink. If you are a drug dealer in Hackney, you can use the kilo of cocaine you own to sell to casual coke users who will snort it and come back a month later—or you can microwave it into crack, which is far more addictive, and you will have your customer coming back for more in a few hours. Prohibition encourages you to produce and provide the more harmful drug.

For Friedman, the solution was stark: take drugs back from criminals and hand them to doctors, pharmacists, and off-licenses. Legalise. Chronic drug use will be a problem whatever we do, but adding a vast layer of criminality, making the drugs more toxic, and squandering £20bn [20 billion British pounds] on enforcing prohibition that could be spent on prescription and rehab, only exacerbates the problem. "Drugs are a tragedy for addicts," he said. "But criminalising their use converts that tragedy into a disaster for society, for users and non-users alike."

Some people imagine that after drug prohibition ends, drug use will become rampant, with Chigwell [a tony London suburb] housewives shooting up next to the chintzy ironing board. No historical analogy is perfect, but with one of his extraordinary, dense statistical analyses, Friedman showed that the fears at the end of alcohol prohibition—that everyone would be glugging gin the moment they could freely buy it—proved to be false. In fact, alcohol use went back to pre-Prohibition levels, and has been falling since, with a brief spike in the Second World War. He also showed that the vast majority of criminals who had bartered in alcohol did not simply move into another form of crime, but went legit when the temptations of such a profitable criminal market disappeared.

Today, an end to drug prohibition seems like a distant fantasy. But in 1924, even as vociferous a wet [an alcohol proponent] as [famed attorney] Clarence Darrow was in despair, writing that it would require "a political revolution" to legalise alcohol in the US. Within a decade, it was done. We are approaching a tipping-point in the drugs debate, when failure becomes undeniable. As we wait, I can still hear Milton Friedman in one of his last interviews: "In the meantime, should we allow the killing to go on in the ghettos? 10,000 additional murders a year? In the meantime, should we continue to destroy Colombia and Afghanistan?"

Neo-prohibitionists Are Again Agitating Against Alcohol

Radley Balko

At the time this article was written, Radley Balko was a policy analyst at the Cato Institute, a libertarian public policy research foundation. He is now a senior editor at Reason *magazine, a publication of the libertarian Reason Foundation. In the following article, published just after the seventieth anniversary of Prohibition's repeal in December 1933, he discusses how new restrictions on the use of alcohol seem aimed at reinstating it by the "back door." Today's agitators against alcohol refuse to learn the lesson of history, he says. Instead of holding drinkers responsible for their actions, they are trying to use legislation and taxation to make liquor less available. This is being done in the name of public health in the belief that it will curb alcohol abuse, but in Balko's opinion it will do more harm than good. Other countries that have liberalized their liquor laws are experiencing a decrease in alcohol-related health conditions and crime, while those that have tightened them continue to battle alcohol-related social ills. The problems of alcohol, he says, lie not with its availability but with the individuals who abuse it.*

"'Tis the season of office holiday parties, family holiday parties, trade group holiday parties and, in Washington, lobbyist holiday parties. And if it's the season of the party, it's also the season of the cocktail—of eggnog aperitifs, Irish coffee and New Year's champagne.

The December just ended also happened to mark the 70th anniversary of the repeal of alcohol Prohibition. For 13 years early last century, a nip of anything but Jack Frost himself might get you fined, or tossed in the tank. Despite the grand

and complete failure that Prohibition was, it's becoming increasingly clear this holiday season that there are a growing number of Scrooges out there who refuse to learn the lessons of history.

A new generation of temperance advocates are again agitating against alcohol. A slew of government organizations, nonprofit groups and "public health" foundations are setting the stage for what you might call a "back door to prohibition."

Organizations such as Mothers Against Drunk Driving, the Center for Science in the Public Interest, and the Center on Addiction and Substance Abuse have advocated for an incremental, multipronged attack to restrict your access to alcohol. They are calling for excise taxes, restrictions on alcohol advertising, tougher public intoxication laws, and laws aimed at holding the alcohol, restaurant and tavern industries liable for alcohol abuse. In short, these neo-prohibitionists aim to use legislation and litigation to control the "environment of alcohol," instead of holding individual drinkers accountable for their actions.

And they're finding success.

New Restrictions

[In 2002–2003], 29 states have either adopted or attempted to pass increases in taxes on alcohol. Several U.S. cities, including Oakland, Baltimore and Cleveland, have either banned alcohol ads on city billboards or severely restricted them. Twenty-two states have imposed restrictions on happy-hour drink specials. Thirty-one have "social host" laws, which hold party hosts (even private parties) liable for the actions of guests who consumed alcohol at private residences. Advocates have indicated that they will use the campaign against tobacco as their model, and that we can soon expect to see litigation aimed at further limiting how and when and where we get our drink. All of these initiatives are advocated under the umbrella of "public health." Curb Americans' access to alcohol, the thinking goes, and you'll also curb alcohol consumption. Curb consumption, and you'll curb the costs on society caused by alcohol abuse. Unfortunately, the evidence suggests otherwise.

First, there's increasing support for the theory that moderate alcohol consumption brings far more good than harm. Recent medical studies have credited moderate consumption with helping to prevent everything from heart disease to pulmonary function to prostate cancer. In 1994, the *Journal of the American Medical Association* editorialized that moderate alcohol consumption could prevent as many as 80,000 American deaths each year. There's also evidence that liberalizing our alcohol laws will do more to minimize the deleterious effects of alcohol than tightening them. The Adam Smith Institute, a London free-market think tank, reports that Scotland has been gradually liberalizing its restrictions on its pubs, to the point where bars there can today stay open around the clock. Scots have begun to drink less as a result, and tend to nurse their drinks over longer periods of time, instead of binging in the hours before the bars close (known in Australia as the "5 o'clock swill"). Alcohol-related arrests are down in Scotland, as are alcohol-related health conditions and injuries.

The Netherlands recently relaxed its liquor laws to allow discotheques and clubs to operate around the clock. The country has since seen a significant reduction in closing-time street crime. Some clubs began running buses to shuttle patrons home. Others now serve breakfast to the hardiest of bar-hoppers. In contrast, the Institute points out, countries that have already enacted the kinds of policies temperance advocates are pushing in the United States (Canada, England and the Scandinavian countries, for example), have continued to battle problems associated with alcohol abuse. Excessive taxation and restrictions on access to alcohol in Britain have created thriving black markets. Scandinavian countries have tried to control alcohol behavior with stringent access laws, and have battled alcohol-related social ills all along the way.

Our lawmakers should learn from Prohibition. This is a country that will drink with the blessing of the law, or will drink in spite of it. As America reflects on 70 years of freedom of libation we should also remember that it isn't the "environment of alcohol" that needs to be held responsible for alcohol abuse, it's the individuals who abuse alcohol.

A Growing Movement Supports Lowering the Drinking Age

Alex Johnson

Alex Johnson is a reporter for MSNBC.com. In the following article he reports on a growing movement to lower the drinking age from twenty-one to eighteen. Both advocates and opponents are concerned about the rise in binge drinking among teenagers. The opponents of lowering the drinking age consider this proof that teens should not be allowed to drink, but the advocates believe that the present law has driven youthful drinking underground where it cannot be controlled, which happened with alcohol use during Prohibition. The evidence shows that it has not stopped teens from drinking, they say; the real problem is that teenagers are not being taught how to drink responsibly, and because they view it as "forbidden fruit" they are more likely to drink to excess than they were before the age was raised. Opponents, on the other hand, claim that setting the drinking age at twenty-one has saved lives.

Over the strong objection of federal safety officials, a quiet movement to lower the legal drinking age to 18 is taking root as advocates argue that teenagers who are allowed to vote and fight for their country should also be able to enjoy a beer or two.

The proposal, which is the subject of a national petition drive by the National Youth Rights Association, has been studied in a handful of states in recent years, including Florida, Wisconsin, Vermont and Missouri, where supporters are pushing a ballot initiative.

Opponents of the idea point to a reported rise in binge drinking as teenagers increasingly turn to hard liquor as proof

Alex Johnson, "Debate on Lower Drinking Age Bubbling Up," MSNBC.com, August 14, 2007. Republished with permission of MSNBC.com, conveyed through Copyright Clearance Center, Inc. www.msnbc.msn.com/id/20249460.

that minors should not be allowed to drink, but proponents look at the same data and draw the opposite conclusion.

"Raising the drinking age to 21 was passed with the very best of intentions, but it's had the very worst of outcomes," said David J. Hanson, an alcohol policy expert at the State University of New York–Potsdam. "Just like during national Prohibition, the law has pushed and forced underage drinking and youthful drinking underground, where we have no control over it."

But Mark Rosenker, chairman of the National Transportation Safety Board [NTSB], countered: "Why would we repeal or weaken laws that save lives? It doesn't make sense."

Different Laws in Different States

As it happens, there is no such thing as a "federal legal drinking age." Many states do not expressly prohibit minors from drinking alcohol, although most of those do set certain conditions, such as its use in a religious ceremony or in the presence of a parent or other guardian.

The phrase refers instead to a patchwork of state laws adopted in the mid-1980s under pressure from Congress, which threatened in 1984 to withhold 10 percent of federal highway funds from states that did not prohibit selling alcohol to those under the age of 21. By 1988, 49 states had complied; after years of court fights, Louisiana joined the crowd in 1995.

Libertarian groups and some conservative economic foundations, seeing the age limits as having been extorted by Washington, have long championed lowering the drinking age. But in recent years, many academics and non-partisan policy groups have joined their cause for a different reason: The age restriction does not work, they say. Drinking has gone on behind closed doors and underground, where responsible adults cannot keep an eye on it.

"It does not reduce drinking. It has simply put young adults at greater risk," said John N. McCardell, former presi-

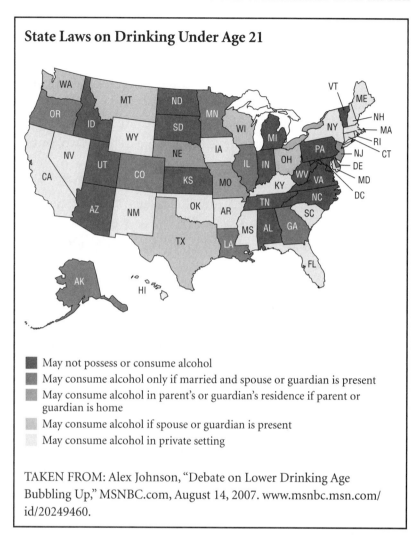

State Laws on Drinking Under Age 21

- ■ May not possess or consume alcohol
- ■ May consume alcohol only if married and spouse or guardian is present
- ■ May consume alcohol in parent's or guardian's residence if parent or guardian is home
- ■ May consume alcohol if spouse or guardian is present
- ■ May consume alcohol in private setting

TAKEN FROM: Alex Johnson, "Debate on Lower Drinking Age Bubbling Up," MSNBC.com, August 14, 2007. www.msnbc.msn.com/id/20249460.

dent of Middlebury College in Vermont, who [in 2007] set up a non-profit organization called Choose Responsibility to push for a lower drinking age.

McCardell offers what he calls a simple challenge:

"The law was changed in 1984, and the law had a very specific purpose, and that was to prohibit drinking among those under the age of 21," he said. "The only way to measure the success of that law is to ask ourselves whether, 23 years later, those under 21 are not drinking."

So are they?

The federal government's National Survey on Drug Use and Health found that in 2005, the most recent year for which complete figures are available, 85 percent of 20-year-old Americans reported that they had used alcohol. Two out of five said they had binged—that is, consumed five or more drinks at one time—within the previous month.

"The evidence is very clear," McCardell said. "It has had no effect."

James C. Fell, a former federal highway safety administrator who is a senior researcher on alcohol policy with the Pacific Institute for Research and Evaluation, acknowledged that "it's not a perfect law. It doesn't totally prevent underage drinking."

But Fell said the age restriction "does save lives. We have the evidence."

Lower Death Rate Disputed

The evidence, widely touted by Rosenker of the NTSB, Mothers Against Drunk Driving and other activist groups, rests in a study by the National Highway Traffic Safety Administration, or NHTSA, which estimated that from 1975 to 2003, higher drinking ages saved 22,798 lives on America's roadways.

"Twenty-five thousand lives is a lot of people to set aside when you're looking at a current problem," said Brian Demers, a 20-year-old student at the Massachusetts Institute of Technology who is a member of MADD's board of directors.

That figure is disputed by proponents of lowering the drinking age. They have questioned the NHTSA study, which did not explain how it arrived at its estimate. Moreover, it counted any accident as "alcohol-related" if any participant was legally drunk—including victims who may not have been responsible for the accident.

"The methodology used has been widely criticized by scholars," said Hanson, of SUNY-Potsdam, who called the report "really more of a guesstimate" that showed only a correlation of numbers, not a causal relationship. In fact, he said, alcohol-related traffic fatalities among minor drivers were already declining before 1984, when the drinking-age measure was passed.

Barrett Seaman, author of "Binge: What Your College Student Won't Tell You," echoed Hanson's assessment, saying, "Those statistics are a little suspicious."

Even so, Rosenker said, alcohol is still the leading cause of death among teenagers in highway crashes.

"The data show that when teens drink and drive they are highly unlikely to use seat belts," he said. "These are the facts, and it would be a serious mistake and a national tragedy to weaken existing drinking age laws."

'Written Out of the Equation'

To McCardell, however, the real problem is that we are not teaching teenagers how to drink responsibly.

Choose Responsibility proposes lowering the drinking age to 18, but only in conjunction with "drinking licenses," similar to driver's licenses, mandating alcohol education for those ages 18 to 21.

"Education works," McCardell said, but "it's never been tried. Now it's mandatory only after you've been convicted of DUI [driving under the influence]. That is not an act of genius."

Choose Responsibility and its allies face a tough task convincing the public. In a Gallup poll released [in August 2007], 77 percent of Americans opposed lowering the drinking age to 18. But Seaman argued that it was the wisdom of the drinker that mattered, not his or her age.

"The problem we have is that since the 21-year-old age limit has been in effect, we have effectively written adults out of the equation, so that they really have nothing to do with young people who are drinking alcohol furtively, viewing alcohol as a forbidden fruit and drinking to excesses that I don't think were evident back in the years before the law was passed," said Seaman, who lived on the campuses of 12 U.S. and Canadian colleges while researching his book.

"If you lower that drinking age—make drinking no longer a forbidden fruit but rather something that younger adults do with older adults who have learned how to handle alcohol responsibly—then you reduce those behaviors rather than increase them," he said.

Appendices

Appendix A

The Amendments to the U.S. Constitution

Amendment I: Freedom of Religion, Speech, Press, Petition, and Assembly (ratified 1791)

Amendment II: Right to Bear Arms (ratified 1791)

Amendment III: Quartering of Soldiers (ratified 1791)

Amendment IV: Freedom from Unfair Search and Seizures (ratified 1791)

Amendment V: Right to Due Process (ratified 1791)

Amendment VI: Rights of the Accused (ratified 1791)

Amendment VII: Right to Trial by Jury (ratified 1791)

Amendment VIII: Freedom from Cruel and Unusual Punishment (ratified 1791)

Amendment IX: Construction of the Constitution (ratified 1791)

Amendment X: Powers of the States and People (ratified 1791)

Amendment XI: Judicial Limits (ratified 1795)

Amendment XII: Presidential Election Process (ratified 1804)

Amendment XIII: Abolishing Slavery (ratified 1865)

Amendment XIV: Equal Protection, Due Process, Citizenship for All (ratified 1868)

The Amendments to the U.S. Constitution

Amendment XV: Race and the Right to Vote (ratified 1870)
Amendment XVI: Allowing Federal Income Tax (ratified 1913)
Amendment XVII: Establishing Election to the U.S. Senate
                     (ratified 1913)
Amendment XVIII: Prohibition (ratified 1919)
Amendment XIX: Granting Women the Right to Vote (ratified 1920)
Amendment XX: Establishing Term Commencement for Congress
                     and the President (ratified 1933)
Amendment XXI: Repeal of Prohibition (ratified 1933)
Amendment XXII: Establishing Term Limits for U.S. President
                     (ratified 1951)
Amendment XXIII: Allowing Washington, D.C., Representation in the
                     Electoral College (ratified 1961)
Amendment XXIV: Prohibition of the Poll Tax (ratified 1964)
Amendment XXV: Presidential Disability and Succession
                     (ratified 1967)
Amendment XXVI: Lowering the Voting Age (ratified 1971)
Amendment XXVII: Limiting Congressional Pay Increases
                     (ratified 1992)

Appendix B

Court Cases Relevant to the Eighteenth and Twenty-first Amendments

Mugler v. Kansas, 1887
The Supreme Court ruled that states have the power to pass and enforce prohibition laws.

Leisy v. Hardin, 1890
The Supreme Court ruled that it is a violation of the Constitution's commerce clause for a state to prohibit the sale of intoxicating liquor brought from another state or country if it is in the original packages or kegs, unbroken and unopened.

Clark Distilling Company v. Western Maryland Railway Company, 1917
The Supreme Court ruled that the Webb-Kenyon Act, which prohibited interstate transportation of liquor that was intended to be sold, used or possessed in a state where that was unlawful, did not conflict with the commerce clause.

Crane v. Campbell, 1917
The Supreme Court ruled that a state could prohibit and punish the possession of intoxicating liquor for personal use.

United States v. Hill, 1919
The Supreme Court upheld the constitutionality of the Reed amendment (to the Webb-Kenyon Act), which prohibited personal importation of liquor into a state that did not allow its manufacture and sale even when the state's own law allowed individuals to bring it in for personal use.

National Prohibition Cases, 1920
In a group of seven cases that challenged the constitutionality of the Eighteenth Amendment, the Supreme Court issued a single opinion overruling the objections and declaring that the amendment was valid.

Jacob Ruppert v. Caffey, 1920

The Supreme Court ruled that although beer containing a mere one-half of 1 percent alcohol was not intoxicating and the Eighteenth Amendment concerned only intoxicating beverages, banning it under the Volstead Act was incidental to the general power to ban beer.

Hawke v. Smith, 1920

The Supreme Court upheld Ohio's ratification of the Eighteenth Amendment over objections that the Ohio Constitution provided for a referendum on the issue by voters, ruling that the federal law set forth in Article V of the U.S. Constitution, which provides specifically for ratification by state legislatures, preempts state laws.

United States v. Simpson, 1920

The Supreme Court ruled that transportation of whiskey by its owner in his own automobile, for his personal use, into a state whose laws prohibited the manufacture or sale of intoxicating liquors for beverage purposes was interstate commerce and violated the Reed amendment.

Dillon v. Gloss, 1921

The Supreme Court ruled that the Eighteenth Amendment went into effect one year from the date its ratification was complete, not from the date its ratification was certified by the Secretary of State, and that convictions for offenses committed during the interval between the two dates were valid.

United States v. Yuginovich, 1921

The Supreme Court ruled that the government could tax liquor even though its production was prohibited, but that tax regulations applying to registered distillers were superseded by the national prohibition law.

Grogan v. Walker & Sons, 1922

The Supreme Court ruled that transportation of whiskey intended as a beverage in bond from Canada through the United States destined to a foreign country, and transshipment of whiskey from one British ship to another in a port of the United States, were forbidden by the Eighteenth Amendment and the National Prohibition Act.

Hawes v. Georgia, 1922
The Supreme Court ruled that a state law providing that a person prosecuted for permitting a still on land occupied by that person was presumed to have known of its presence did not violate due process of law.

United States v. Lanza, 1922
The Supreme Court ruled that for defendants to be prosecuted under both the federal Volstead Act and a state law forbidding manufacture, sale, and transportation of liquor did not violate the constitutional ban on double jeopardy (being tried twice for the same offense).

Cunard Steamship Co. v. Mellon, 1923
The Supreme Court ruled that the Eighteenth Amendment applied to both domestic and foreign ships while in U.S. waters, but not elsewhere, and that therefore liquor carried into U.S. waters by foreign ships could be seized even if enroute to another country.

Hester v. United States, 1924
The Supreme Court ruled that seizure of liquor in plain view in open fields after federal agents had trespassed on a defendant's land did not violate the Fourth Amendment. This case established the "open fields" doctrine, which has been applicable in search and seizure cases ever since.

James Everard's Breweries v. Day, 1924
The Supreme Court ruled that Congress had authority to forbid prescription of malt liquor for medicinal purposes, even though the Eighteenth Amendment prohibited traffic in intoxicating liquors only "for beverage purposes."

Carroll et al. v. United States, 1925
In this landmark case, the Supreme Court ruled that warrant-less searches of automobiles suspected of transporting liquor do not violate the Fourth Amendment.

Samuels v. McCurdy, 1925
The Supreme Court ruled that states could prohibit home possession of alcohol acquired before Prohibition went into effect, although the national prohibition law allowed it.

Selzman v. United States, 1925
The Supreme Court upheld the federal government's power under the Eighteenth Amendment to regulate denatured alcohol, which is intended only for industrial use, on the grounds that people might try to drink it (as some did, although it was poisonous and often fatal).

Steele v. United States, 1925
The Supreme Court ruled that search warrants could be issued to prohibition agents even though they were employees, rather than civil officers, of the government.

Hebert v. Louisiana, 1926
The Supreme Court ruled that the power of states to prosecute defendants for violation of state liquor laws was not derived from the Eighteenth Amendment and therefore was independent of whatever action was taken against a defendant under federal law.

Lambert v. Yellowly, 1926
The Supreme Court ruled that Congress had the power to regulate prescription of wine and spirituous liquor for medicinal purposes, even though they were considered to have more legitimate medical uses than the malt liquor banned by *James Everard's Breweries v. Day*.

Murphy v. United States, 1926
The Supreme Court ruled that even if a defendant were acquitted of maintaining a common nuisance under the prohibition law—that is, a place where liquor was manufactured,

sold, or kept—the separate provision of the law allowing the Court to enjoin occupancy of the place for one year was intended as prevention, not punishment, and therefore still applied.

United States v. Katz, 1926

The Supreme Court ruled that the provision of the Prohibition Act requiring a person who manufactured, purchased for sale, or transported any liquor to make a record of the transaction in detail applied only to those authorized to deal in nonbeverage liquor; it was not intended to add a second offense to the crimes of bootleggers who failed to record their own illegal deals.

Van Oster v. Kansas, 1926

The Supreme Court ruled that forfeiture of property used in violation of a state's liquor prohibition laws could apply to property (e.g., an automobile) of an innocent owner who entrusted its possession and use to the wrongdoer, and the owner was not entitled to a jury trial.

Ford v. United States, 1927

The Supreme Court ruled that British vessels could be boarded and seized if there was reasonable cause to believe they were involved in importation of liquor into the United States and that their officers could be prosecuted not only for illegal importation, but for conspiracy, even if they had not personally entered the United States.

Gambino v. United States, 1927

The Supreme Court ruled that state troopers were in effect federal agents when they arrested violators of the Volstead Act.

Marron v. United States, 1927

The Supreme Court ruled that although under the Fourth Amendment a search warrant does not allow seizure of items not named in the warrant, officers do not need a warrant to arrest persons committing a crime in their presence or to seize items connected to that crime, and that therefore records seized during the arrest of someone found selling liquor were legally taken.

United States v. Lee, 1927
The Supreme Court ruled that the Coast Guard had the right to search and seize an American vessel on the high seas if there was probable cause to believe that the law was being violated, and that failure of the government to seize the boat or the liquor it carried did not make the search illegal.

United States v. Sullivan, 1927
The Supreme Court ruled that gains from illicit traffic in liquor were subject to income tax, and that the Fifth Amendment did not excuse a defendant from failing to file a tax return.

Donnelley v. United States, 1928
The Supreme Court ruled that Prohibition officers could be prosecuted for failing to report violations of the law.

Grosfield v. United States, 1928
The Supreme Court ruled that the purpose of the provision of the National Prohibition Act authorizing an injunction against occupation and use of premises where liquor was manufactured was not punitive, but preventive, and that therefore, lack of criminal participation by the owner was not a defense.

Olmstead v. the United States, 1928
In this landmark case, the Supreme Court ruled that wiretapping did not constitute a search or seizure under the Fourth Amendment and that evidence against bootleggers thus obtained was admissible even where wiretapping was against state law.

United States v. Farrar, 1930
The Supreme Court ruled that purchasing liquor for beverage use was not a crime, and that wording in the Prohibition Act

making it illegal to purchase it without a permit was meant to apply only to persons lawfully entitled to deal in liquor for nonbeverage purposes.

United States v. Sprague, 1931

The Supreme Court ruled against defendants indicted under the National Prohibition Act who claimed that the Eighteenth Amendment had not been properly ratified because it should have been done by constitutional conventions rather than state legislatures.

Various Items of Personal Property v. United States, 1931

The Supreme Court ruled that an illegal distillery could be seized by the government under the principle that civil forfeitures are actions against the property itself rather than against the owner. This case set an important precedent that the Court has cited in recent cases involving the war on drugs.

United States v. Constantine, 1935

The Supreme Court ruled that the federal government could not impose an extra tax on illegal liquor transactions because such a tax was actually a penalty—if it were intended for enforcement of the Eighteenth Amendment, it had to end with the adoption of the Twenty-first, and the federal government cannot impose penalties for violations of state laws.

State Board v. Young's Market Co., 1936

The Supreme Court ruled that under the Twenty-first Amendment a state can exact a license fee for the privilege of importing beer from other states, although prior to that amendment this would have been illegal under the commerce clause.

Mahoney v. Joseph Triner Corp., 1938

The Supreme Court ruled that under the Twenty-first Amendment the equal protection clause of the Fourteenth Amendment is inapplicable to imported liquor, and that states can therefore discriminate among brands in issuing licenses to import.

Collins v. Yosemite Park & Curry Co., 1938

The Supreme Court ruled that the Twenty-first Amendment does not confer upon a State the power to regulate the importation of liquor into territory such as national parks over which it has ceded exclusive jurisdiction to the federal government.

Ziffrin, Inc. v. Reeves, 1939

The Supreme Court ruled that the Twenty-first Amendment gives states the right to absolutely prohibit the manufacture of intoxicants, their transportation, sale, or possession, irrespective of when or where produced or obtained or the use to which they were to be put, despite any contrary provisions of the commerce clause, and to adopt regulations for enforcing this.

Duckworth v. Arkansas, 1941

The Supreme Court ruled that transportation of liquor through a state without a permit in violation of state law is covered by general commerce laws. But one justice argued that "if the Twenty-first Amendment is not to be resorted to for the decision of liquor cases, it is on the way to becoming another 'almost forgotten' clause of the Constitution."

Wisconsin v. Constantineau, 1971

The Supreme Court ruled that although the Twenty-first Amendment gives states broad powers to deal with problems such as excessive drinking, for the police to post without warning a notice in liquor outlets that no liquor may be sold or given to a particular person because of his behavior is an unconstitutional violation of due process.

California v. LaRue, 1972

The Supreme Court ruled that under the Twenty-first Amendment, states have the right to refuse liquor licenses to establishments offering sexually explicit entertainment even though to forbid such entertainment by law would violate the First Amendment right to free speech.

Craig v. Boren, 1976

The Supreme Court ruled that although the Twenty-first Amendment gives the power to regulate liquor sales to the states, it does not override the equal protection clause of the Fourteenth Amendment, and that states therefore cannot set different drinking ages for men and women.

Capital Cities Cable, Inc. v. Crisp, 1984

The Supreme Court ruled that a state law preventing cable television operators from carrying advertisements for alcoholic beverages was invalid under Federal Communications Commission (FCC) regulations, and that the Twenty-first Amendment does not supersede the FCC's jurisdiction because the law did not further the purpose of the amendment.

South Dakota v. Dole, 1987

The Supreme Court ruled that although the Twenty-first Amendment gives the right to regulate the sale of alcohol to the states, it does not prevent the federal government from setting conditions involving that sale, such as denying federal highway funds to states that do not comply with its suggested minimum drinking age.

Rubin v. Coors Brewing Co., 1994

The Supreme Court ruled that the federal government cannot restrict free speech by prohibiting the display of alcohol content on beer labels, despite its claim that this facilitates state efforts to regulate alcohol under the Twenty-first Amendment.

44 Liquormart, Inc. v. Rhode Island, 1996

The Supreme Court ruled that state restrictions on advertising the price of liquor are not authorized by the Twenty-first Amendment and that they violate First Amendment protection of free speech.

Granholm v. Heald, 2005

The Supreme Court ruled that although the Twenty-first Amendment gives states the power to ban all direct shipments of liquor to consumers, states may not discriminate against out-of-state wineries by allowing only shipments from within the state.

For Further Research

Books

Herbert Asbury, *The Great Illusion: An Informal History of Prohibition*. Garden City, NY: Doubleday, 1950.

Edward Behr, *Prohibition: Thirteen Years That Changed America*. New York: Arcade, 1996.

Jack S. Blocker, *American Temperance Movements: Cycles of Reform*. Boston: Twayne, 1989.

Eric Burns, *The Spirits Of America: A Social History of Alcohol*. Philadelphia: Temple University Press, 2004.

Edward Butts, *Outlaws of the Lakes: Bootlegging and Smuggling from Colonial Times to Prohibition*. Holt, MI: Thunder Bay Press, 2004.

Sean Cashman, *Prohibition: The Lie of the Land*. New York: Free Press, 1981.

Norman H. Clark, *Deliver Us from Evil: An Interpretation of American Prohibition*. New York: Norton, 1976.

Joe L. Coker, *Liquor in the Land of the Lost Cause: Southern White Evangelicals and the Prohibition Movement*. Lexington: University Press of Kentucky, 2007.

Larry Engleman, *Intemperance: The Lost War Against Liquor*. New York: Free Press, 1979.

Allan S. Everest, *Rum Across the Border: The Prohibition Era in Northern New York*. Syracuse, NY: Syracuse University Press, 1978.

J.C. Furnas, *The Life and Times of the Late Demon Rum*. New York: Putnam, 1965.

Richard F. Hamm, *Shaping the Eighteenth Amendment: Temperance Reform, Legal Culture, and the Polity, 1880–1920*. Chapel Hill: University of North Carolina Press, 1995.

Paul R. Kavieff, *The Violent Years: Prohibition and the Detroit Mobs*. Fort Lee, NJ: Barricade Books, 2007.

K. Austin Kerr, *Organized for Prohibition: A New History of the Anti-Saloon League*. New Haven, CT: Yale University Press, 1985.

John Kobler, *Ardent Spirits: The Rise and Fall of Prohibition*. New York: Putnam, 1973.

David E. Kyvig, *Repealing National Prohibition*. Chicago: University of Chicago Press, 1979. Available online at www.druglibrary.org/schaffer/history/rnp/rnptoc.htm.

David E. Kyvig, ed., *Law, Alcohol, and Order: Perspectives on National Prohibition*. Westport, CT: Greenwood, 1985.

Mark E. Lender and James K. Martin, *Drinking in America: A History*. New York: Free Press, 1982.

Michael A. Lerner, *Dry Manhattan: Prohibition in New York City*. Cambridge, MA: Harvard University Press, 2007.

Philip P. Mason, *Rumrunning and the Roaring Twenties: Prohibition on the Michigan-Ontario Waterway*. Detroit: Wayne State University Press, 1995.

Mark H. Moore and Dean R. Gerstein, eds., *Alcohol and Public Policy: Beyond the Shadow of Prohibition*. Washington, DC: National Academy Press, 1981.

Kenneth M. Murchison, *Federal Criminal Law Doctrines: The Forgotten Influence of National Prohibition*. Durham, NC: Duke University Press, 1994.

Catherine Gilbert Murdock, *Domesticating Drink: Women, Men, and Alcohol in America, 1870–1940*. Baltimore: Johns Hopkins University Press, 1998.

Thomas R. Pegram, *Battling Demon Rum: The Struggle for a Dry America, 1800–1933*. Chicago: Ivan R. Dee, 1998.

Kenneth D. Rose, *American Women and the Repeal of Prohibition*. New York: New York University Press, 1996.

Vivienne Sosnowski, *When the River Ran Red: How California's Legendary Winemakers Fought the Epic Battle to Survive Prohibition*. New York: Palgrave Macmillan, 2009.

Mark Thornton, *The Economics of Prohibition*. Salt Lake City: University of Utah Press, 1991.

Periodicals

Radley Balko, "Zero Tolerance Makes Zero Sense," *Washington Post*, August 9, 2005.

Sean Flynn, "Should the Drinking Age Be Lowered?" *Parade*, August 12, 2007.

Mike Gray, "Perils of Prohibition," *Nation*, September 20, 1999.

David Greenburg, "Tanked: How New York Dealt with the 'Noble Experiment,'" *Bookforum*, June/July 2007.

Linda Greenhouse, "Justices Pick Apart Ban on Wine Sales from State to State," *New York Times*, December 8, 2004.

David Harsanyi, "Prohibition Returns! Teetotaling Do-Gooders Attack Your Right to Drink," *Reason*, November 1, 2007.

Susan Kinzie and James Hohmann, "Lower Drinking Age Is Criticized," *Washington Post*, August 21, 2008.

Jackson Kuhl, "Eight Million Sots in the Naked City: How Prohibition Was Imposed on, and Rejected by, New York," *Reason*, November 2007.

David E. Kyvig, "Women Against Prohibition," *American Quarterly*, 1976.

Margot Opdycke Lamme, "Tapping into War: Leveraging World War I in the Drive for a Dry Nation," *American Journalism*, no. 4, 2004.

Charles Lane, "Justices Reject Curbs on Alcohol Sales," *Washington Post*, May 17, 2005.

Caryn E. Neumann, "The End of Gender Solidarity: The History of the Women's Organization for National Prohibition Reform in the United States, 1929–1933," *Journal of Women's History*, vol. 9, 1997.

Stanton Peele, "Alcohol Denial: The Government's Prejudice Against Alcohol Is a Hangover from Prohibition," *National Review*, August 11, 1997.

Jonathan Saltzman, "Juror's Challenge Raises Legal Issues," *Boston Globe*, August 8, 2008.

Andrew Stuttaford, "Killjoy Was Here," *National Review*, December 31, 2003.

Jacob Sullum, "Prohibition's Past and Present," *Reason*, July 1997.

Elizabeth M. Whelan, "Perils of Prohibition: Why We Should Lower the Drinking Age to 18," *Newsweek*, May 29, 1995.

David Witwer, "The Rise of Gangsters," *Cobblestone*, April 2006.

Internet Sources

Brandon Arnold, "Legacy of Prohibition Lives on in Maryland," December 5, 2007. www.cato.org/pub_display.php?pub_id=8829.

Radley Balko, "Back Door to Prohibition: The New War on Social Drinking," *Cato Institute Policy Analysis*, December 5, 2003. www.cato.org/pub_display.php?pub_id=1360.

Donald Boudreaux, "Prohibition Politics," *Pittsburgh Tribune-Review*, July 25, 2007. www.pittsburghlive.com/x/pittsburghtrib/s_518872.html.

Ernest H. Cherrington, Facsimile of address to Congress delivered on December 10, 1913, calling for a Prohibition amendment to the Constitution. Brown University Library. http://dl.lib.brown.edu/repository2/repoman.php?verb=render&id=1108062094359375.

Kristin Daly, "Same Problem—Same Solution," Law Enforcement Against Prohibition (LEAP). www.leap.cc/cms/index.php?name=Content&pid=44.

Richard M. Evans, "How Alcohol Prohibition Was Ended," www.druglibrary.org/think/~jnr/endprohb.htm.

Fabian Franklin, *What Prohibition Has Done to America*. New York: Harcourt Brace, 1922 (full text). www.druglibrary.org/schaffer/history/e1920/what_prohibitiontoc.htm.

Jami Goodman, Evan Feuerstein, and Jared Kastriner, "Prohibition, the Forgotten Crusade," YouTube. www.youtube.com/watch?v=szntim2j9Rg.

Richard Hamm, "American Prohibitionists and Violence, 1865–1920." www.druglibrary.org/schaffer/history/prohibit.htm.

Frederic J. Haskin, "Prohibition," from *The American Government*, 1923. www.druglibrary.org/schaffer/HISTORY/prohibtn.htm.

HistoryCentral.com, Volstead Act, 1920 (full text). www.multied.com/documents/Volstead.html.

Theodore B. Lacey, "The Supreme Court's Fluctuating Reaction to National Prohibition in Fourth Amendment Decisions from 1920–1933." http://web.princeton.edu/sites/jmadison/awards/ 2005-Lacey_Thesis.pdf.

Library of Congress, "The Dry Years: Selected Images Relating to Prohibition from the Collections of the Library of Congress." www.loc.gov/rr/print/list/073_dry.html.

Declan McCullagh, "Prohibition Redux?" CNET News, November 8, 2004. http://news.cnet.com/ Prohibition-redux/2010-1071 _3-5442340.html.

Peter McWilliams, "Prohibition: A Lesson in the Futility (and Danger) of Prohibiting," from *Ain't Nobody's Business If You Do*, Prelude Press, 1996. www.mcwilliams.com/ books/books/aint/402.htm.

Carl H. Miller, "Prohibition and the Will to Imbibe." www.beerhistory.com/library/holdings/ prohibition_1.shtml.

National Commission on Law Observance and Enforcement, "Report on the Enforcement of the Prohibition Laws of the United States" (Wickersham Commission Report on Alcohol Prohibition), January 7, 1931. www.druglibrary.org/Schaffer/Library/studies/wick.

National Commission on Marihuana and Drug Abuse, "History of Alcohol Prohibition." www.druglibrary.org/ schaffer/library/studies/nc/nc2a.htm.

New York Times, "Prohibition Repeal Is Ratified," December 5, 1933. www.nytimes.com/learning/general/onthisday/ big/1205.html.

Online Library of Drug Policy, "Did Prohibition Reduce Alcohol Consumption and Crime?" www.druglibrary.org/Prohibitionresults.htm.

J. Petrillo, "Rum Running in the North Country During Prohibition," Adirondack Roots Project, 2001. http://faculty.plattsburgh.edu/jay.petrillo/ Background%20Info%20page.htm.

Bob Ramsey, "A History of U.S. Drug Laws; or, How Did We Get into This Mess? Part 1: 1898–1933," Drug Policy Forum of Texas, June 9, 2004. www.dpft.org/history.html.

Paul Craig Roberts, "Repeal of Today's Prohibition Is Past Due," *Milwaukee Journal*, January 21, 1995. http://findarticles.com/p/articles/mi_qn4207/ is_19950120/ai_n10181985.

K. Jacob Ruppert, "In Re John Barleycorn: The Role of NYCLA in the Repeal of Prohibition," *New York County Lawyer*, October 2005. www.jacobruppert.com/ prohibition.html.

Nancy Galey Skogland, "The *I'm Alone* Case: A Tale from the Days of Prohibition," *University of Rochester Library Bulletin*, Spring 1968. www.lib.rochester.edu/ index.cfm?PAGE=1004.

Jacob Sullum, "Prohibition Was Not an Awful Flop," *Reason* Hit and Run blog, September 7, 2005. www.reason.com/blog/show/110854.html.

Mark Thornton, "Alcohol Prohibition Was a Failure," *Cato Institute Policy Analysis*, July 17, 1991. www.cato.org/pub_display.php?pub_id=1017.

Time, "Fizz Water," August 6, 1928. www.time.com/time/printout/0,8816,787465,00.html.

U.S. Senate Judiciary Committee Hearings on National Prohibition, April 5 to April 24, 1926. www.druglibrary.org/schaffer/history/e1920/ senj1926/default.htm.

Web Sites

Alcohol Problems and Solutions,
www2.potsdam.edu/hansondj/index.html. A large site maintained by Professor David J. Hanson, professor emeritus of sociology, State University of New York–Potsdam, who has done extensive research on alcohol. It contains many detailed articles about the history and effects of Prohibition.

Amethyst Initiative, www.amethystinitiative.org. An association of college and university presidents who advocate lowering the drinking age to eighteen in order to reduce binge drinking among students.

Anti-Saloon League, www.wpl.lib.oh.us/AntiSaloon. A site maintained by the Westerfield Public Library in Ohio, which in 1973 acquired the organization's buildings and papers.

Digital History, http://www.digitalhistory.uh.edu. An American history site created by the University of Houston that includes an article about Prohibition.

Internet Archive, www.archive.org. A nonprofit Internet library offering permanent access for researchers, historians, and scholars to historical collections that exist in digital format. It contains a number of texts from the Prohibition era, including some entire books.

New York Times Archive, http://query.nytimes.com/search. A complete archive of articles published in the *New York Times*. No charge to read those earlier than 1923 or later than 1986; others require a fee. To search for Prohibition Era articles click on "Go to advanced search," choose "NYT Archive 1851–1980" in drop-down box, and then click "Custom date range."

Prohibition Repeal, www.prohibitionrepeal.com. A site celebrating the seventy-fifth anniversary of Prohibition's repeal on December 5, 2008. It contains detailed material about the Prohibition era.

Temperance and Prohibition, http://prohibition.osu.edu. A site maintained by the Ohio State University Department of History, containing articles, pictures, and cartoons on the topic.

Index